Archecive
½ 2 (9)

D1460179

of *Scarbrough* Viscount and Baron *Lumley* of *Lumley* Castle Viscount
the Counties of *Northumberland* Durham Town and County of *Newcastle* upon
the Gentlemen of the Bed Chamber, and one of his Ma.^tes Most Honble Privy Councill.

Enchanted Forest

ABOVE *North-west view of Stansted,
drawn and engraved by W. Pink, 1853.*
OVERLEAF *Stansted today –
the Main Entrance.*

Enchanted Forest
THE STORY OF STANSTED IN SUSSEX

LORD BESSBOROUGH
WITH
CLIVE ASLET

Weidenfeld & Nicolson
London

Contents

To the memory of my mother,
who cared for the house and garden,
and for my wife,
who has continued to do so.

Copyright © Lord Bessborough & Clive Aslet, 1984

First published in Great Britain in 1984 for
the Stansted Park Foundation by
George Weidenfeld & Nicolson Ltd
91 Clapham High Street, London sw4 7TA

All rights reserved. No part of this publication
may be reproduced, stored in a retrieval system,
or transmitted in any form or by any means
electronic, mechanical, photocopying, recording
or otherwise without the prior permission of the copyright
owners.

ISBN 0 297 78491 9
Designed by Joyce Chester
Edited by Russell Ash
Typeset and printed in Great Britain by
BAS Printers Limited, Over Wallop, Hampshire

Arms of some of the principal owners of Stansted shown in the windows of the Chapel. LEFT *to* RIGHT : *Roger de Montgomerie, Earl of Arundel ; Henry II ; the d'Aubigny and Fitzalan Earls of Arundel ; the Lumleys ; the Earl of Halifax ; Richard Barwell ; Lewis Way ; George Wilder.*

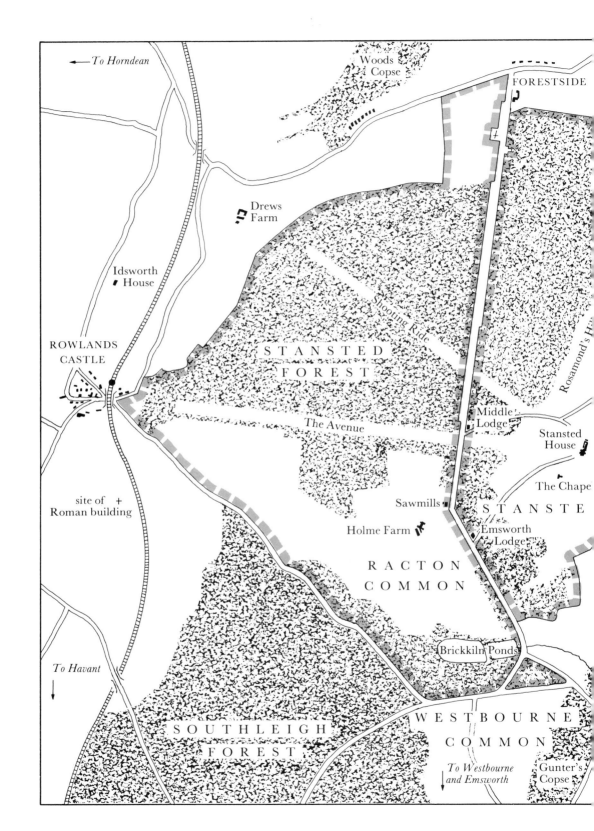

← To Horndean

Woods
Copse

FORESTSIDE

Drews
Farm

Idsworth
House

Shooting Ride

ROWLANDS
CASTLE

S T A N S T E D
F O R E S T

Rosamond's H.

Middle
Lodge

Stansted
House

The Avenue

The Chape

site of +
Roman building

Sawmills

S T A N S T E

RACTON
COMMON

Holme Farm

Emsworth
Lodge

To Havant

Brickkiln Ponds

W E S T B O U R N E

SOUTHLEIGH
FOREST

C O M M O N

To Westbourne
and Emsworth

Gunter's
Copse

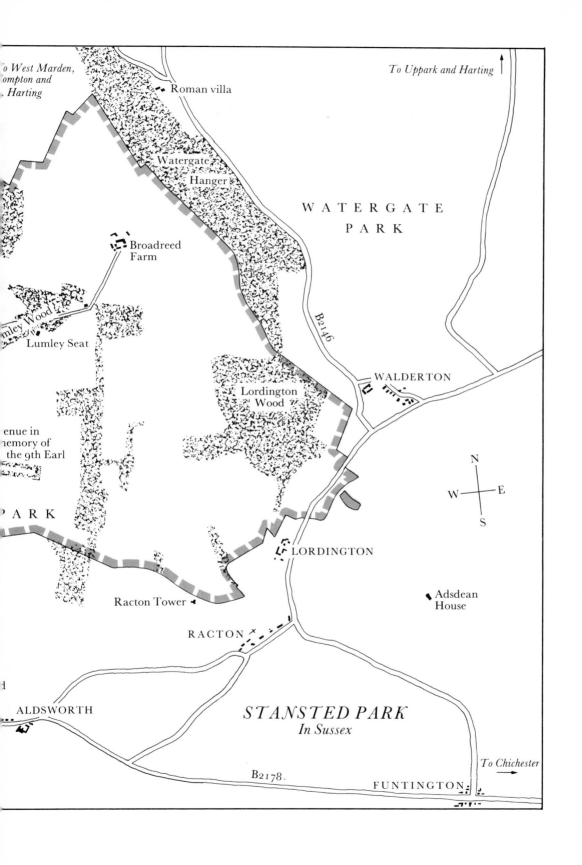

To West Marden,
ompton and
Harting

Roman villa

To Uppark and Harting

Watergate
Hanger

WATERGATE
PARK

Broadreed
Farm

B2146

...mley Wood

Lumley Seat

Lordington
Wood

WALDERTON

...enue in
...nemory of
the 9th Earl

N
W E
S

...PARK

Racton Tower

LORDINGTON

Adsdean
House

RACTON

ALDSWORTH

STANSTED PARK
In Sussex

To Chichester

B2178

FUNTINGTON

Preface

Enter these enchanted woods,
You who dare.
(George Meredith, *The Woods of Westermain*, 1883)

THERE IS SOMETHING about an English country house or even the site of a house with an ancient history which may inspire man's nobler as well as sometimes his baser instincts. So it has been with Stansted; and so it has been with many other houses up and down the country. It is not of Hampton Court and Hatfield or Nostell and Uppark (itself only a few miles from Stansted) that we think in this respect but of hundreds of other houses with perhaps less claim to fame from the historical or the strictly architectural point of view. Each of these houses tells its own story; and when such a house is situated, as Stansted is, in the midst of an ancient enchanted forest which still exists today, its romance is irresistible. Although for some 700 years the place was handed down by direct descent, the remarkable variety of owners in later years gives the story an added interest.

For these reasons I have felt impelled to bring together the various strands of history and threads of tradition which have woven themselves about the place since the earliest days. It has not been an easy task as these threads have from time to time been blown away like cobwebs from a dusty ceiling; when, for example, the five-hundred-year tenure of the Earls of Arundel came to an end at the close of the sixteenth century; again during the Civil War and again after two hundred years of Lumley ownership – to say nothing of more recent changes. Finally the fire in 1900 destroyed all the records that remained in the house at the time. I have therefore to a considerable extent been able only to consult what might be described as secondary sources. Contemporary rolls, chronicles and accounts have, it is true, yielded some information, but practically no local archives exclusively relating to Stansted are in existence.

It was in 1923, as a boy of ten, that my father and mother told me they must come to a decision about finding a house where they could hang the family pictures which had been saved when the family house, Bessborough, near Waterford in Ireland, had been burnt down. They had already seen some sixty houses and I was given a copy of the latest *Country Life* and asked to help make the final choice. There in the early pages

8

The Middle Lodge.

I saw a beautiful photograph of Stansted from the avenue and told my parents that was my choice and they agreed.

I am particularly indebted to my late father's article, 'Stansted and its Owners', which appeared in the *Sussex County Magazine* of August 1952, his pamphlet on *Stansted Chapel*, printed in March 1954, and his booklet on *The Society of Stansted Players*, last printed in 1937. I have made further use of all the sources mentioned in these publications including *John Keats: The Living Year* by Robert Gittings (1954) published by Messrs William Heinemann Ltd, to whom I am indebted for permission to quote certain passages; an article by A. Cecil Piper in *Records of Chichester* by T. G. Willis (1928), *The Ways of Yesterday* by A. M. W. Sterling (1930) and an article, 'Notable Owners of Stansted Park', by Admiral Chambers in the *Sussex County Magazine* (November and December 1933).

I have in addition also consulted works not directly used by my father, i.e., James Dallaway's *County of Sussex* (1815), T. W. Horsfield's *County of Sussex* (1835), *History and Antiquities of Arundel* by M. A. Tierney (1834), *The House of Arundel* by Pym Yeatman (1888), *The Dukes of Norfolk* by John Martin Robinson (1982), *Records of the Lumleys* by Edith Milner (1904), T. H. Mee's *Bourne in the Past* (1913), the letters of John Keats

9

in *The Complete Works* (Vol. V) edited by H. Buxton Forman (1901 and 1923), not forgetting the volume on *The Rape of Chichester* in *The Victoria County History of Sussex* by L.F. Salzman (1953), together with many of the sources mentioned therein, such as *Honors and Knights' Fees* (1923–24) by William Farrer, R.W. Eyton's *Court, Household and Itinerary of Henry II* (1878), the *Pipe Rolls* of the various reigns and the relevant volumes of the *Sussex Archaeological Collections* as well as other local sources. I have of course also referred to appropriate articles in the *Dictionary of National Biography*, the *Encyclopaedia Britannica* and *The Complete Peerage*. For the dispute between John Fitzalan and St Richard of Chichester see also the preface to my play, *Like Stars Appearing* (1953).

I am most grateful to the Right Honourable, the late Earl of Scarbrough for assistance in preparing that part of the book which concerns the Lumleys; to the late Admiral the Hon. Sir Herbert and Lady Meade-Fetherstonhaugh of Uppark; to the late Mrs Eleanor B. Hankey, a daughter of George and Mary Wilder, who lived at Stansted for twenty-five years at the end of the last century, and to Thomas Nelson and Sons for allowing me to quote a verse from the last poem in *The Four Men* by Hilaire Belloc (1911).

I am also much indebted to the late Mr W.C. Browning, former Secretary of the Stansted Park Estate Company, to Mr John F. Fleming, the well-known international antiquarian of New York City, to Mr William Van Lennep, Curator of the Theatre Collection of the Houghton Library of Harvard University and not least to Mr F.W. Steer, former County Archivist in Chichester, and his successors, Mrs Patricia Gill and Mr Peter Wilkinson, for valuable assistance in compiling this work.

Above all, I must thank Sir Brian Batsford for all his assistance in bringing out in 1958 the first edition of the book on which this volume is based; Clive Aslet for his additional research as well as his three articles about Stansted in *Country Life* in February 1982 and also Francis Russell at Christie's for his help in compiling the picture list.

Finally, I should like to thank Russell Ash for his work as editor of this book, Joyce Chester for designing it, and Felicity Luard, Poppy Smith and everyone else at Weidenfeld & Nicolson who guided it through all stages of its production.

I must, however, assume full responsibility for the accuracy of all the statements made, from sunrise to sunset.

1 *The Sun Rises*

The woods shall to me answer and my echo ring.
Edmund Spenser, *Epithalamion*, 1595.

'HERE IS THE beginning,' I said, as we swept aside the leaves and revealed the tessellated pavement, the Roman mosaic, in the woods of Watergate Hanger. My wife and I were barely two miles from the house at Stansted; and since these Roman remains have now disappeared and no others found nearer by we cannot claim for certain that Roman legions marched down the long avenue at Stansted, but I like to think they did. However, it was clear from the mosaic at Watergate that there must have been Romans in the neighbourhood. Six miles away towards Chichester is the Roman Palace at Fishbourne which was discovered in 1960. My wife was indeed one of the earliest enthusiastic observers of these excavations. At all events there seems no doubt, as Professor Barry Cunliffe has said, quoting T. W. Horsfield, that Roman patricians had villas in this part of West Sussex.

Otherwise there is little that can be said about the earliest days until we come to late Saxon times when Stansted or *Stanestede* with its extensive forest (part of what was already in the twelfth century called the Forest of Bere) represented the whole or part of the sixteen hides of Stoughton which were held by Earl Godwin of King Edward the Confessor. A hide was a holding supporting a family and varying in size from 40 to 120 acres.

'Cupid on a dolphin' mosaic at Fisbourne.

II

It was sometimes defined as the amount of land that could be tilled by one plough in a year.

Stansted itself enjoyed paramount rights from the earliest antiquity. Earl Godwin, the father of King Harold, married his daughter Edith to King Edward with whom he was dining when he died of apoplexy in 1053. In the previous year Godwin made his famous descents on the Isle of Wight and may well have used Stansted as his base for this purpose.

After Harold had been defeated by the Normans in 1066, the same sixteen hides were temporarily attached to Westbourne. In the Domesday Book they were included in the Hundred of Bourne. They consisted mainly of forest and, as will be seen, something in the nature of a hunting lodge seems to have been built there in the twelfth century. At that time the Earls of Arundel certainly made Stansted one of their residences. There they held their forest courts and had hunting rights, 'free chase and free warren', from Arundel to Rowlands Castle. As the old Sussex tradition has it:

> Since William rose and Harold fell
> There have been Earls of Arundel.

Roger de Montgomery, Earl of Arundel, commonly known as Earl Roger, had commanded the centre at the Battle of Hastings and has been described as foremost among the conquerors of England. But his successor, Earl Robert de Bellême, that 'monster of iniquity', was attainted, and forfeited the estates in 1113 mainly for stirring up Robert of Normandy to invade England. But many other charges against him were also made.

The Earldom of Arundel then passed to the Albinis, or the d'Aubignys as perhaps they should be more properly called. They were a distinguished family. The first d'Aubigny Earl was William surnamed 'the strong hand' from the legend that he pulled out the tongue of a lion which had been let loose to destroy him by Adeliz, the Queen Dowager of France. She was supposed to have done this out of jealousy for his having rejected her for her namesake in England. On William d'Aubigny's marriage to Adeliz, the Queen Dowager of England and widow of Henry 1, he acquired with her in 1138 the Castle and Honour of Arundel which had been settled on her in dower and which included Stansted. William seems at the same time to have assumed the style of Earl of Arundel. He sheltered the Empress Maud at Arundel but ever after remained loyal to King Stephen. In 1141 he attested a charter of Stephen as Earl of Sussex and may be presumed to have been so created after Stephen regained his freedom. He was also at other times styled Earl of Chichester but throughout this time he appears to have been more generally known as Earl of Arundel.

2 *Henry the Second and His Sons*

WILLIAM D'AUBIGNY WAS influential in arranging the treaty of 1153 whereby the Crown continued with Stephen for life, though the inheritance was secured to Henry II. William, held in great esteem by Henry II, was one of the embassy to Rome in 1163 and to Saxony in 1168. He was also in command of the royal army in Normandy in 1173 against the King's rebellious sons, and a few weeks later assisted at the defeat near Bury St Edmunds of the Earl of Leicester who had invaded Suffolk with his Flemings. He died in 1176 and was succeeded by his son, also called William.

In view of Henry II's friendship with the first Earl William it is not surprising to learn that, according to the Chronicle of Benedict of Peterborough, the King spent a week at Stansted in 1177. This was seven years after the murder of Saint Thomas Becket, four years after his penance at Canterbury and very soon after he obtained from the Pope partial recognition of his constitutions which included a provision requiring an oath of fealty from all Englishmen. In May of that year the government of Ireland was remodelled and the King's youngest son, John, was proclaimed Lord of Ireland. At this time Henry was at the height of his powers. Alfred Duggan in *The Devil's Brood* describes him from 1175 to 1182 as being 'the greatest monarch in Christendom. He ruled England absolutely . . . was obeyed in Wales and Ireland and taken seriously as overlord of Scotland. In . . . Normandy, Acquitaine, Anjou and Maine, he could enforce his wishes . . .'

It was between 1173 and 1175 that there appeared the illuminated manuscript Gospel Book of Henry the Lion which was sold at Sotheby's in 1983 for some eight million pounds. It is in this superb volume that there appears what is probably the only contemporary portrait of Henry II with his daughter Matilda and her husband, Henry the Lion, Count of Saxony and Duke of Bavaria, whom she married in 1168. Henry the Lion has been described as one of the wealthiest and most romantic figures in European history, who personally owned not only Saxony and Bavaria, but also Austria and considerable parts of Italy, Scandinavia and Western Russia. Whether Henry the Lion and Matilda visited Stansted cannot be definitely ascertained, but it is quite possible that they did, since Henry sided with Henry II against Becket, must have met Matilda a year or two before Becket's murder and spent part of the years 1181–5 in exile in the court of Henry II in England. Like his father-in-law, he could well have used Portsmouth harbour – that is, Stokes Bay near Portchester – in crossing the Channel and brought Matilda to meet her father at Stansted.

In July 1177, the King had intended to set out for Normandy from Stokes Bay but the winds were not favourable and he came instead to Stansted. He arrived on 10 July and two days later received news there from France that the Papal Legate threatened to place the kingdom under an interdict unless he would permit the consummation of the marriage of his son, Richard, with Alice, the daughter of the King of France, who was in Henry's constant care and almost certainly with him at Stansted. Henry consulted Richard of Dover, Becket's successor as Archbishop of Canterbury, and the Bishops of Ely, Exeter and Chichester, all of whom were with him at Stansted, and it was resolved that the prelates should appeal to the Pope against the Legate.

R. W. Eyton in his *Court, Household and Itinerary of Henry II* says that 'the Legate's threat, the perpetual diplomacy with France on the subject of the Princess Alice and the persistent, nay aggravated, disaffection of Prince Richard support the suspicion and allegation that Henry had debauched the affianced bride of his son'. But despite the looseness of his personal morals and his violent and capricious temper, Henry II was without doubt a remarkable legislator and administrator with a high sense of his responsibilities. He also had a strong love of justice and commanded the respect of the most upright of the English bishops, including, I believe, those who were with him at Stansted in the summer of 1177.

Another very different matter settled by Henry II at Stansted, in consultation with the Bishops, concerned the Royal Chaplaincy of Bosham which was surrendered by the wrongful incumbent, Arnulf, Bishop of Lisieux, and restored to Bartholomew, Bishop of Exeter. Yet another problem resolved there referred to the grant of permission to the Jews to have their own cemetery outside the walls of every city. Until then the Jews' only burial ground was in London. Henry II spent in all eight days at Stansted. An old wound caused by the kick of a horse gave him trouble and he returned to Winchester to obtain treatment. In September of the same year he concluded his arbitration between the Kings of Castile and Navarre and made a special vow to go on a crusade to the Holy Land. But of course he never went.

Two years later, in 1179, Richard and Ralph, the King's falconers, were at Stansted; and in 1181 Silvester and his comrades were looking after the King's birds in the park. During the next three years it appears from

Richard I, from a
medieval manuscript.

The Great Roll of the Pipe that large sums were spent on the King's buildings at Stansted: viz: £81. 15s. 5d. in 1181–2 for the King's *nove camera* (new chamber), £34. 14s. 9d. in 1182–3 for the chamber and kitchen, and £9. 6s. 10d. in 1183–4 for repair of the *domibus* (house). The total expenditure for the three years was thus £125. 17s. 10d., which represents many thousands of pounds in today's money. This suggests that Henry II may have paid a number of other unrecorded visits to Stansted in his later years. He was certainly at Portsmouth again in 1188 waiting to embark on his last campaign against King Philip of France with whom his son, Richard the Lionheart, was then in league. Whether or not Henry visited Stansted again at this time I do not know, but J. H. Round in his introductions to the volumes printed by the *Pipe Roll Society* instances Stansted as one of the houses which the King had built in addition to his castles and refers to it as a place which he visited for hawking on the downs.

The nearest of the King's castles was the old Roman fort of Portchester, the rebuilding of which appears to have been completed a few years before the work was done on the King's building at Stansted. It is a fair surmise that towards the end of his reign the King must have travelled from one to the other on more than one occasion. He is, indeed, said to have ridden as much as forty miles a day. From his visits to Portchester, Chichester and Bosham the King must have come to know the country surrounding Stansted well, and it was no doubt his appreciation of it that induced him to come to an arrangement with the first and perhaps also the second d'Aubigny Earl to build his own hunting lodge there.

I like to think that my own ancestor, John FitzPonson, who according to Sir John Ponsonby in his book, *The Ponsonby Family*, was hereditary Barber and Surgeon to Henry II, may also have visited Stansted at this time and cut or curled the head of this famous Plantagenet. On the Ponsonby shield are still emblazoned 'three combs argent' which record the office held by the first of the Ponsonbys to come over to England from Normandy. No doubt John FitzPonson was well known to the second d'Aubigny Earl of Arundel, of whom there is little to be said except that in addition to receiving possession of the Castle and Honour of Arundel he was in 1191 made *Custos* (keeper) of Windsor Castle and in 1194 one of the receivers of the money raised for the King's ransom. He evidently died soon after this.

According to the chronicle of Roger de Hoveden, King Henry's son, Richard the Lionheart, hunted deer and wild boar at Stansted in April 1194. This was during his short stay in England after his imprisonment in Germany on returning from the Crusades and before he left England again for the last time – in May – to defeat Philip Augustus and to restore his authority in Aquitaine.

Richard's second coronation had taken place at Winchester on 17 April. Five days later he left Winchester for Portsmouth where a fleet of over a hundred ships had been assembled. But as Philip Henderson points out in his biography of Richard, storms delayed the departure of the Royal party for more than three weeks. After waiting at Portsmouth for a few days the King went to Stansted to hunt. However in his absence his Welsh and Brabantine mercenaries came to blows and many were killed. The King had, therefore, to interrupt his hunting and return to Portsmouth to pacify them. After three more inactive days at Portsmouth, a place which Richard is believed to have found very tedious, he put to sea but was soon turned back by the bad weather and spent a further eight days chafing at Portsmouth and no doubt longing to go hunting at Stansted. It was only on the ninth day that the whole fleet finally set sail.

OPPOSITE *Henry II (standing, third from right) at the coronation of Matilda and Henry the Lion.*

OPPOSITE *Stansted House – the East Front.*
RIGHT *King John, drawn by Matthew Paris.*

At the beginning of the thirteenth century parts of Stansted were (with Racton) the subject of suits between Ralph Sanzaver and William, son of Ilbert of Rakinton. But the royal interest in the place continued. The second d'Aubigny Earl's son was also called William, and this third William was a favourite of King Henry's youngest son, King John, whose concession of the Kingdom to the Pope in May 1213, he witnessed and whom he accompanied to Runnymede in June 1215. King John was at Stansted in January 1214, just before he set out to invade Poitou. He was there again on more than one occasion a year later in January 1215, probably just before or very soon after the barons had demanded their liberties of him while he was staying at the Temple in London – that is to say some six months before he left for Runnymede with William d'Aubigny and was finally forced to sign the *Magna Carta*. On his last visit to Stansted the King ordered a cask of wine from Aldingbourne for consumption that evening at the house. William, the third d'Aubigny Earl, died in 1220, and the estate passed to his son Hugh, who married Isabel, daughter of William de Warenne, Earl of Surrey. He died in 1243 and she, as a widow, became a friend of Matthew Paris the famous chronicler and monk of St Albans whose part I took in my play *Like Stars Appearing* which was performed at Glyndebourne in 1953.

3 *The Fitzalan Earls of Arundel*

IN 1244 STANSTED was part of the dower granted by Hugh d'Aubigny (the last Earl of Arundel of his line) to his sister and co-heir, who was also called Isabel and became Countess of Arundel in her own right. She married the first John Fitzalan and Stansted passed to their son, John, who became Lord (and newly so-called Earl) of Arundel and Chief Butler to the King. The manor was no doubt included in the lands recognized by Henry III as belonging to him and among those which in fact pertained to Richard of Wyche (later Saint Richard) as Bishop of Chichester, but to which Henry III forbade him access until after his consecration by the Pope. I have already described the character of his dispute with St Richard in the preface to my play *Like Stars Appearing*, which I have already mentioned. This John Fitzalan, who must have hunted very frequently at Stansted, took part in the Welsh War in 1258 and, although sometimes in league with the barons, fought on the royal side at the Battle of Lewes in 1265 and was taken prisoner with the King.

In 1283, during the minority of Richard, the third Fitzalan Earl, the Manor of Stansted was granted with Westbourne to the Abbey of Vale Royal in aid of their works. Fourteen years later, in May 1297, soon after Balliol's surrender of Scotland, Edward I passed through Stansted Forest on his way from Bedhampton to Arundel. This visit followed his stay at Portsmouth where he was making preparations for his expedition to Bruges to help the Count of Flanders against the French.

Between 1302 and 1330 Stansted formed part of the Manor of Westbourne. In 1306 during the minority of Edmund, the fourth Earl, it is recorded that William de Whiteway trespassed in the park and was convicted before the treasurer and barons of the Exchequer. This evidently meant that de Whiteway, a parker at Stansted, had done some damage while King Edward I, in the last year of his long reign, held the property as guardian of the young Earl. As far as can be ascertained it seems that judgement was only executed a year or two later in the following reign – that of Edward II – and that de Whiteway was then committed to the Tower of London and remained there in prison over four years. But the exact nature of his offence remains obscure. Dr Mee in *Bourne in the Past* thinks it may have been of the same kind as those of which Richard, the fifth Earl, complained in 1335, 'that divers persons had broken into his

Saint Richard,
Bishop of Chichester.

parks at . . . Stansted . . . hunted there and carried away deer' and 'that the Dean of Chichester and others cut down his trees . . . and carried them away with other goods'. In view of the excellent relations which exist with more recent Deans of Chichester this complaint calls for no comment from me. Evidently de Whiteway's offence may have involved the unauthorized sale or disposal of timber or other produce of the land.

Edmund, the fourth Earl, attended the coronation of Edward II but for a long time was opposed to him and particularly to Piers Gaveston. However, in 1321 he changed sides. He was Warden of the Welsh Marches in 1325 and was eventually captured in Shropshire by the Queen's party and beheaded in 1326. It seems unlikely that he spent very much time at Stansted. At any rate in a survey made in the year after he was beheaded Stansted is described as comprising 'a hall, two chambers with a Chapel, a kitchen and a chamber over the gate, a stable and a cowshed, worth

Stansted Chapel, on the site of the earliest
recorded buildings.

nothing, beyond reprises'. These buildings were no doubt those which had been built or restored for Henry II and were presumably on and around the site of the present Chapel.

For nearly a hundred years after this survey I have been able to trace no records relating to Stansted. The Fitzalan Earls continued but how often they came to Stansted is not known. Those who were interested in hawking and hunting or performed naval duties at Portsmouth must have stayed there frequently.

4 *Admirals of the West*

RICHARD, CALLED 'COPPED Hat', Fitzalan succeeded as fifth Earl in 1331 and took a distinguished part in the war with France. As Admiral of the ships at Portsmouth he must have been at Stansted a good deal. He later became Admiral of the West and commanded the second division at the Battle of Crécy. He was on unhappy terms with William de Lenne, the Bishop of Chichester who cited him at the Papal Court, but Edward III supported him, and the Bishop's temporalities were seized. Richard was immensely wealthy, advanced considerable sums to Edward III and greatly enlarged Arundel Castle. There is no evidence of his having made any important changes at Stansted.

Richard Fitzalan was succeeded in 1376 by his son, another Richard (the sixth in line), who bore the Crown at the coronation of Richard II in 1377, was made Admiral of the West and South and, in 1386, of all England. He too must have been well known at Stansted although he was often in the wars. He gained a brilliant naval victory over the allied French, Spanish and Flemish fleets off Margate in 1387, saved Southampton from French assault and in 1388 was made Governor of Brest. He was with John of Gaunt on the expedition to St Malo, and with the Duke of Gloucester later took an active part against Richard II, who in 1388 was entirely in the Duke's power. In 1394 he was pardoned for all his political offences but three years later was treacherously seized, tried at Westminster as a traitor, arrayed in scarlet and beheaded on Tower Hill. Later he was revered as a martyr and placed in the company of the Saints.

His son, Thomas Fitzalan, restored as seventh Earl in 1400, was for a time a ward of the Duke of Exeter, by whom he was harshly treated. After escaping from him and living on the Continent for some time he returned in 1399 with the Duke of Lancaster (afterwards Henry IV) who made him Governor of the Tower of London. In company with Hotspur he fought with moderate success against the Welsh and took a leading part in the siege of Harfleur. Henry V made him High Treasurer and Warden of the Cinque Ports. I find that according to a subsidy levied in 1411–12: 'Thomas, Earl of Arundel, and Surrey has Arundel Castle, and has manors, lands, etc., viz., the Manor of Bourne with Stanstede, Walderton and the hundred, members of that Manor: £53.'

Thomas married Beatrice, the natural but probably legitimized

Effigies of Thomas, 7th Fitzalan Earl of Arundel, and his wife, Beatrice, natural daughter of King John of Portugal, in the Fitzalan Chapel, Arundel.

daughter of King John I of Portugal, known as the Great. The King had two natural children by Ines Pires. The first was Alfonso, who became Count of Barcelona and married the daughter of Nuno Alvares Pereira, the Constable of the Realm and later the first Duke of Braganza; and the second was Beatrice, who married Thomas, Earl of Arundel, in 1405. However, Thomas died ten years later and Beatrice married another English nobleman, Baron Irchenfield. He died four years later in 1419, but when Beatrice passed away she was buried with her first husband. Ines Pires bore these natural children before the King's marriage to Phillippa of Lancaster, daughter of John of Gaunt. That marriage produced several remarkable princes including Henry the Navigator and Joao who was Constable of the Realm as well as their sister Isabel who married Philip Le Bon when he founded the Order of the Golden Fleece and who was the mother of Charles the Bold.

From 1422 to 1455 it is recorded that Stansted was held in dower by Eleanor, widow of John, the eighth Earl. This John Fitzalan had been *de jure* Lord Mautravers and was in the French wars in 1415. It may well be that during this year there was some military activity around Stansted in preparation for the embarkation from Portchester of Henry v's army for Agincourt. John Fitzalan himself died in 1421 but his widow, Eleanor, lived on until 1455. Their son John, the ninth Earl, was at the coronation of Henry vi in Paris in 1431 and so greatly distinguished himself in the French wars that he became known as 'The English Achilles'. He was severely wounded and taken prisoner in 1435 and died soon afterwards. His son, Humphrey, the tenth Earl, died three years later in his tenth year, and the earldom passed to his uncle, William. This William, the eleventh Earl, was defeated with the Yorkists in 1461 and ten years later was made Constable of Dover Castle and Warden of the Cinque Ports. He served at the coronations of Richard iii and Henry vii, founded the so-called 'Arundel Mass' and died in 1487.

5 *Tudor Earls*

IT HAS ALWAYS been alleged that the old house at Stansted was built by William Fitzalan's son, Thomas, Lord Mautravers (who later became the twelfth Earl), in about 1480, but from the survey already mentioned and the references in the Pipe Rolls to Henry II's buildings it is evident that there were earlier buildings on the same site. Some stone in the present Chapel dates from the twelfth century, which seems to confirm that there were buildings there in Henry II's time if not earlier. The 1480 house was a castellated and turreted brick building which must have been on somewhat the same plan as the buildings shown in Grimm's drawing.

Grimm's drawing is dated 1782, but under Bonnor's print of the same drawing its date is given as 1778. Under the Bonnor print the old house is described as showing 'what was once the mansion of the Earls of Arundel, now degraded to the stables and barns of a more modern seat, probably from its style erected about the time of Charles I'. This rebuilding

The old house, drawn by S. H. Grimm, 1782.

Henry, the last Fitzalan Earl of Arundel by Holbein

presumably took place just before the Civil War during which, as will be seen below, it no doubt suffered damage as a result of the military occupation. The 'more modern seat' mentioned in the description of the Bonnor print presumably referred to the house built for Lord Scarbrough in 1686 and of which we shall hear more later. When this house was built on the new site the old buildings around the Chapel were no doubt allowed to fall into disrepair and used only as farm buildings.

After the references to Stansted in the middle of the fifteenth century some hundred years again elapse until we learn that Edward VI was there in 1552 at the age of fifteen. This visit took place immediately after the English Prayer Book first began to be used in Divine Service and about a year before he died of consumption in 1553. During this time the Fitzalan Earls continued to play their part at Court and in affairs of state. Thomas, the twelfth Earl, married Margaret Woodville, the sister of Elizabeth who was Edward IV's Queen. As Lord Mautravers he attended the coronation in 1485 of Richard III, when he bore the Rod with the Dove (one of the most ancient ornaments of English kingship) and of his niece, Elizabeth, the daughter of Edward IV and Queen Consort of Henry VII. In 1489 he was made Warden of the New Forest which in those days was joined with the Forest of Bere in which Stansted is situated. Thomas rebuilt West-bourne parish church and must have spent a considerable time at Stansted but not a great deal is known of him. He had a son, William, the thirteenth Earl, who also bore the Rod with the Dove at the coronation of Anne Boleyn in 1533. His grandson, Henry, the last Fitzalan Earl, was named after his godfather, Henry VIII, who was one of his sponsors in person.

Henry was perhaps the most illustrious of all the Fitzalan Earls. In 1544 he was 'Marshal of the Field' against the French and distinguished himself at the taking of Boulogne. He was Lord Chamberlain from 1546 to 1550 and one of the Council of Twelve named by Henry VIII in 1547. The Council was disgusted by the Protector Somerset, and Fitzalan urged his dismissal; but Warwick later became jealous of the influence of Arundel, who was suspected of using his position as Lord Chamberlain to enrich himself. This was never proven. Henry acted as High Constable at the coronation of Edward VI. However, in 1551 he was fined and imprisoned in the Tower for more than a year as a result of the hostility of the Duke of Northumberland. He took revenge on the Duke by pretending to join him in setting up Lady Jane Grey as Queen and then betraying him to Queen Mary and arresting him at Cambridge. His offices continued under Queen Mary and Queen Elizabeth whom, indeed, he aspired to marry. This aspiration led to a violent quarrel with Leicester, and he became one of Elizabeth's several disappointed suitors. On being rejected in 1564 he resigned all his offices, and in 1579 he died. His picture probably by Holbein is in the Marquis of Bath's collection. He was also painted by Sir Anthony More. Some sources describe the picture in the great hall at Parham (which is barely twenty miles from Stansted) as also being of him; but the late Christopher Hussey pointed out that this picture is, in fact, of his son, Henry Fitzalan, Lord Mautravers, who died of fever in 1556 at the early age of nineteen while returning from an embassy to the King of Bohemia, thus predeceasing his father by some twenty-three years.

6 Lumleys and Queen Elizabeth

AT THE DEATH of Henry Fitzalan in 1579 Stansted descended with West-bourne to John, Lord Lumley, in right of his wife, Jane, who was Henry's daughter. As stated in John Martin Robinson's quincentennial history, *The Dukes of Norfolk* (1982), her sister, Mary, married Thomas Howard, fourth Duke of Norfolk. During the reign of Edward VI John Lumley had obtained an Act of Parliament providing that he and his heirs should enjoy the dignity and estate of baron. As such he attended the funeral of Edward VI and, with his wife, Jane, the coronation of Queen Mary in 1553. On that occasion he was made a Knight of the Bath. He fulfilled various judi-

John Lumley by Van der Meulen.

cial functions and as a Lord of Parliament attended the Queen's marriage in July 1554. On Elizabeth's accession he attended her on her journey from Hatfield to London and sat as a commissioner to try claims to service at her coronation. In this capacity he acted again forty-five years later for the coronation of James I.

For fifty years, from 1559 until his death, John Lumley was high Steward of the University of Oxford. In 1564 he undertook to deal with the Florentines to secure payment of a debt of £11,000 to Henry VIII. He and his father-in-law, Henry Fitzalan, Earl of Arundel, became responsible to the Queen, who gave the Florentines a discharge. But their failure to pay the promised instalments is said to have greatly embarrassed Lord Lumley until the end of his life. He was the sole executor and legatee of his father-in-law, Henry Fitzalan, who had already in 1566 given him all the goods he then possessed. By this deed he gave him in addition the greater part

Mary Lumley by
Van der Meulen.

of his manors and lands, which included Stansted, in consideration 'of his great travaile and paines taken for me and about my business and affaires during all the time sithens he was firste knowne to me, and for the payment of my debtes he hath soulde the most parte of his own lands and patrimony, and hath bound himself and his frendes in divers bonds and great summes of money'.

Before the death of his father-in-law, Lumley became involved with him in intrigues and plots for the restoration of the Catholic religion and the marriage of the Queen of Scots to the Duke of Norfolk. For this he was arrested and lodged in the Tower for some two-and-a-half years. Later he acted as commissioner in several state trials including those of Mary, Queen of Scots, in October 1586, and Lord Essex in February 1600.

Despite these affairs of state John Lumley seems to have been able to spend a certain amount of time at Stansted. From one of his estate accounts in 1581 it appears that 'wild beasts' were transferred from Goodwood and East Dean to Stansted at about that time. Queen Elizabeth herself came to Stansted at the end of August 1591. She was entertained at Sutton Place in Surrey on her way into Sussex and after visiting Dorking, Horsham, Wiston and Ashington proceeded westward through Parham, Pulborough and probably Petworth to Cowdray which she left on 21 August. She then came to Stansted on her way to Portsmouth where she arrived on 31 August. She must have been amused to see the house which only twelve years previously had belonged to one of her suitors, Henry Fitzalan, and to meet his son-in-law, the new owner. The Queen is said on arrival at Stansted to have cried with perhaps not altogether unexpected humour: 'Stand steed.' George Augustus Walpoole in *The New British Traveller* (1782) states the the place derived its name from these words; but as will have been seen above the place had been called Stanstede or 'stone place' from the earliest days.

Queen Elizabeth was at Stansted during the year in which she supported the claim of Henry of Navarre to the French Crown and the year in which Shakespeare was writing his first plays, *Love's Labour's Lost* and *Romeo and Juliet*, the first of which was performed by the Stansted Players in the Stansted Theatre three hundred and fifty years later. From another account of Lord Lumley dated 1587 relating to 'the carriage of the Queen' in the county of Sussex it appears that she may also have been at Stansted earlier, that is to say at about the time of Drake's dash upon Cadiz during the year preceding the invasion of the Spanish Armada in 1588. Her feelings as she drove through the forest may well be imagined.

7 The Civil War and Charles II

JANE LUMLEY, DAUGHTER of the last Fitzalan Earl, died childless in 1576. When, therefore, her husband, John Lumley, died in 1609 (the same year as the catalogue of his famous library was completed) he was succeeded by his cousin, Sir Richard Lumley, and the last connection with the Earls of Arundel had gone. They must have hunted and lived at Stansted for some 500 years. John Lumley married secondly Elizabeth, daughter of Baron d'Arcy. She was greatly praised for having all 'the virtues of modesty, truth and conjugal love'. In 1614 she is recorded as being the patron of Westbourne Church. She survived her husband and died in about the year 1617. In her will she referred to Stansted in the following terms; 'And my will is that Matthewes and his sonne have the same charge of Stansted and of these lands and libertyes and woodes in Sussex . . . which heretofore and now presently they have, carrying themselves as they ought to doe.'

Sir Richard Lumley, who was brought up by one Richard Lewkenor,

Sir William Waller, the Parliamentary general who took Stansted in 1644.

31

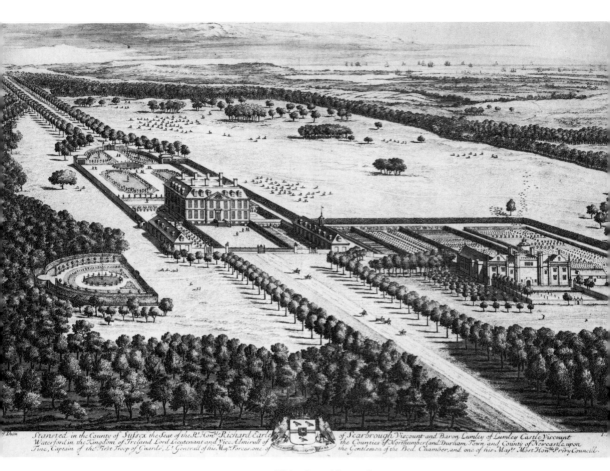

Kip's view of Stansted, 1724.

married first Frances, widow of William Holland of Chichester and daughter of Henry Shelley of Warminghurst. They evidently spent a good deal of time at Stansted. Between 1620 and 1624 their children, Anne, Richard and Julia, were baptised in Westbourne Church and Frances herself was buried there in 1626, as also was her son, Thomas, who died with her in childbirth. Richard had been created Viscount Lumley of Lumley Castle, County Durham, and was a staunch Royalist. He made Lumley Castle a garrison and held a command in the West when Bristol was surrendered to the Parliamentary forces in September 1645.

Stansted had a sorry time during the Civil War. It was occupied first by the Royalists and then by the Parliamentarians. In December 1643 Lord Hopton sent cavalry to attack the house. Then in 1644 the Parliamentary General, Sir William Waller, took the place with '2000 horse and foot with two drakes' (a kind of small cannon) and largely

A recent aerial view.

destroyed the castellated building of which the only remains are that part
of the Chapel as it stands today. This Richard Lumley was among the
'compounders' of 1655 and was heavily fined. He signed the declaration
before the meeting of the Restoration Parliament. According to contemporary records Lumley compounded 'for woods in Stansted Forest,
and a warren on which no value was set . . . because the herbage belongs
to the petitioner, the tenants and other inhabitants'. Richard Lumley died
in 1661 and was buried at Cheam in Surrey. His son, John, who had married Mary, the daughter and co-heiress of Sir Henry Compton, prede-
ceased his father in 1658 and therefore never succeeded to the viscountcy.
The estate passed to his son, another Richard, who at eight years old thus
became the second Viscount.

After the Restoration conditions improved and this Richard Lumley
prospered under Charles II. The King himself must have passed Stansted

OPPOSITE *The West Dining Room, with portraits of William, 2nd Earl of Bessborough (right) and his wife, Caroline Cavendish, by Liotard (left), and Lady Jane Brabazon by Zucchero (centre).* LEFT *Charles II, after Adriaen Hanneman.*

in his grandfather's time before his escape to France in October 1651, in the bark procured by Colonel George Gunter, but young Richard Lumley would only have been one year old at the time. Colonel Gunter was the well-known cavalier who owned Racton and after whose family the copse by the Aldsworth pond is still named.

William Harrison Ainsworth in his historical novel, *Ovingdean Grange*, maintains that Colonel Gunter coming from Racton in the early morning, and King Charles riding from Hambledon, in fact met in 'the central avenue of Stansted Forest'. Although young Richard's father or grandfather may have been in residence, Ainsworth maintains that they did not go into the house 'but skirting the moss-grown palings . . . shaped their course towards the forest which lay further to the west'. In a Racton manuscript it is stated that when the party 'came near Lord Lumley's house at Stansted it was considered that the greatness of the number of the horse might possibly raise some suspicion' and that Colonel Gunter was then dismissed with thanks. This is confirmed in a footnote to a tract by Colonel Gunter published in *Flight of the King* by Allen Fea (1908).

Whether or not the King entered Stansted House, the Lumleys must certainly have been among his supporters. The second Richard Lumley was educated as a Roman Catholic, was Master of the Horse to Charles

II's Queen, Catherine of Braganza, and in 1684 became her Treasurer. He was created Baron Lumley of Lumley Castle in 1681, although, since there was no Parliament, his introduction to the Lords did not come until 1685. It was his troop of Sussex militia and Hampshire horse which captured Lord Grey and the Duke of Monmouth in the New Forest a few days after the battle of Sedgemoor in 1685. But he became dissatisfied with James II's policy, laid down his commission, and in 1687 became a Protestant. He then entered into correspondence with the friends of William of Orange.

However, this second Richard Lumley cannot have fared badly during the four years of James II's reign. According to James Dallaway's *Western Division of Sussex* (1815), regrettably the earliest source for a date, Richard began in 1686 to build a house at Stansted at 'prodigious expense'. It was the first on this site and in a very different style from the old castellated building on the Chapel site.

He was formerly believed to have employed the architect William Talman, who was to become Comptroller of Works to William III in 1689. The new Stansted closely resembles nearby Uppark at Harting – so closely indeed that the Kip views of the two houses have sometimes been confused. These were published in 1724 in the *Nouveau Theatre de la Grand Bretagne*. Both houses have a similar arrangement of stables and offices, those at Uppark, however, being at the side rather than the front of the house. Both are in the Dutch style. Talman is also said to have been the architect of Uppark. But politically it is implausible that both houses should have been from the same hand, since Lord Grey at Uppark was one of Monmouth's closest associates. Indeed it was he who commanded Monmouth's cavalry at Sedgemoor against Lumley's troop. In his monograph on Talman published in 1982, John Harris considers that Stansted is too plain to be by Talman, lacking the touch of idiosyncracy that is the hallmark of the authenticated works. He suggests that Robert Hooke, the curator of experiments to the Royal Society and a friend of Wren, is a more likely candidate – but again evidence is lacking. The uncertainty about the architect is frustrating, since it was one of the most distinguished houses of its age, prefiguring those of William III's court; and Kip's engraving shows that the garden was of equal interest.

OPPOSITE *The Music Room, with pictures of Vere, 9th Earl of Bessborough, painted by de Laszlo during the First World War, and opening the Canadian Parliament in Ottawa, by Richard Jack.*

8 *The First Lord Scarbrough*

IN 1688 RICHARD, second Viscount Lumley, was one of the seven influential Englishmen who signed the invitation to William of Orange 'to bring over an army and secure the infringed liberties' of England. In 1689 King William, who had become a friend and fellow campaigner, made him a Privy Councillor, then in 1690 first Earl of Scarbrough. In that year Lumley fought at the Battle of the Boyne and contributed largely to the final Jacobite defeat. After the battle, a royal warrant caused '20 carbines 8 pair of pistolls to be issued for the use of Our first Troop of Guards commanded by our Rt trusty ... Richard Earle of Scarbrough, & likewise 8 strapt Fuzees for the grenadiers of the said Troop' to replace those lost in action. He was made a Major-General two years later and became Lieutenant-General in 1694. He must have preferred William III's lack of ostentation to Charles II's flamboyant immorality and James II's political and religious bigotry. We hear little of him during Queen Anne's reign as he was presumably living in retirement at Stansted and Lumley Castle. However in 1716, two years after the accession of George I, he became Chancellor of the Duchy of Lancaster and the following year Vice-Treasurer of Ireland. He died in 1721. John Macky, in *Characters of the Court of Great Britain*, wrote of him: 'He is a Gentleman of very good sense, a great lover of the Constitution of his country, and an improver of Trade, and his Genius lay very much this way; a handsome man, of a brown Complexion, turned fifty years old.'

Also in 1721 my own ancestor, Colonel William Ponsonby, who was also a supporter of William of Orange and greatly distinguished himself at the siege of Londonderry in 1688, was created Baron Bessborough. In 1722 he was raised to the title of Viscount Duncannon. His son, Brabazon, who became Privy Councillor in Ireland and Commissioner of Revenues, was made the first Earl of Bessborough by George II in 1739.

It is worth noting that the first Lord Scarbrough's brother, Henry Lumley, a most distinguished soldier, also had ties with West Sussex. He served throughout the wars of William III and Anne. He became a Colonel in 1692, Brigadier-General in the following year and was at the siege of Namur in 1695, after which he also became Major-General. He was MP for Sussex in 1701 and 1702, General and Governor of Jersey in the following year and then fought consecutively at Blenheim, Ramilles, Oudenarde

The 1st Earl of Scarbrough,
by Wissing.

and Malplaquet. The Lumley tapestries which were dispersed from Stansted after the fire of 1900, bought back by my father and myself and now hanging at Stansted, are a fitting memorial to him. They depict Marlborough's campaigns including that of the battle of Wymendaal (1709) and were given to him by Queen Anne.

In 1715, Henry Lumley became MP for Arundel and must then have been a frequent visitor to Stansted. He spoke for the Government on the army in December 1717, but a few days later, on the public breach in the royal family, he sold his regiment for about £9,000 when his nephew, Lord Lumley, was forced to sell his own for adhering to the Prince of Wales.

It is recorded that William III – less than three years after he was crowned – visited the house in February 1692 during the same month as the massacre of the Macdonalds at Glencoe. The King had indeed sanctioned vigorous treatment of the Scottish rebels. At that time Lumley, by then Lord Scarbrough, who had become a Major General, continued to serve with the King in Flanders until the Peace of Ryswick in 1697 when he retired from the Army.

The next royal visit to Stansted was that of the Prince of Wales, later

George II, who arrived on 25 September 1716. 'The next morning', according to a breathless passage in Rapin and Tindal's *History of England* (1725–31), the king 'proceeded to Portsmouth, and having viewed the fortifications, docks, yards and magazines, reviewed the regiments there, and went on board the guard-ship and bomb-ship, dined at Lieut. General Erles', and returned in the evening to Stansted, where Archdeacon Boucher, one of the Canons Residentiary of Chichester, accompanied by the Prebendaries and Vicars of that Cathedral, with many of the neighbouring clergy, were presented to him by Lord Lumley. On the 27th, about nine in the morning, the prince left Stansted and on a common near Rake reviewed Wynn's Dragoons.' This was not long after the suppression of the Jacobite insurrection in the north to which the first Lord Scarbrough contributed.

The Prince of Wales' father, George I, who spoke no English at all, came to Stansted in August 1722, at about the time when Sir Robert Walpole acceded to power and some seven months after the second Earl of Scarbrough had succeeded his father. On 31 August the King was there presented with an address from the Corporation of Chichester. It was handed to him by the Mayor, the Recorder, Sir Thomas Miller and others of the City Council who were introduced to the King by the first Duke of Richmond, then Lord of the Bedchamber. The Duke was the natural son of Charles II and Louise de Queroualle, Duchess of Portsmouth in England and Duchess d'Aubigny in France. He had been created Duke at the age of three and had later purchased Goodwood because of his interest in hunting. He became a Catholic while living with his mother in France, but in 1692 he was received into the Church of England and made his peace with William III as others had done. He died at Goodwood in 1723 at the age of fifty-one, that is to say in the year after he received George I at Stansted.

It is possible that the second Earl of Scarbrough, who had only recently succeeded to his title (he was the first surviving son of the first Earl and also called Richard), was not personally present on this occasion. He is not recorded as being so, and it was no doubt because of his absence that the honours were performed by the Duke of Richmond.

In 1724 Daniel Defoe, who was then writing *Tour thro' the Whole Island of Great Britain* and active as a somewhat shady Whig spy, came to look at Stansted and was suitably impressed. The author of *Robinson Crusoe*, who has been called the 'father of English journalism', gives us the following description: 'From Chichester the road lying still west passes in view of the Earl of Scarbrough's fine seat at Stansted, a house seeming to be

The Staircase, showing one of the tapestries of Marlborough's campaigns.

a retreat, being surrounded with thick woods, through which there are the most pleasant agreeable Vistos [vistas] cut that are to be seen anywhere in England particularly because through the west opening, which is from the front of the house, they sit in the dining room and see the town and harbour of Portsmouth, the ships at Spithead and also at St Helens; which when the Royal Navy happens to be there, as often happened in the late war, is a most glorious sight.'

Due to the profusion of planting and particularly the height of the beech trees today it is not now possible to see Portsmouth from the house.

A view of the avenues through the forest, from the roof of the House.

Emsworth Harbour and Thorney Island are clearly visible from the south front, and from the roof the Isle of Wight and Bosham can also be seen. However, from Lumley Seat to the north-east of the house a complete panorama from Chichester to the Isle of Wight can be admired. It is worth interpolating here that when I took Sir John Betjeman to visit Ewen and Nicky Macpherson at Lumley Seat, he walked out on to the terrace and fell to his knees as though in prayer, exclaiming, 'Tennyson's Mount!' It was a very fine day and this highest point on the Isle of Wight could clearly be seen above the trees in the arboretum at Stansted. It is clear from Defoe's description that at the time of his visit the dining room at Stansted House must have been in the south-west corner of the house which now contains the library. Of the house described by Defoe all that remains today is the cellar which is composed of six bays in two adjoining ranges of quadripartite vaulting. They are carried on circular stone pillars with moulded capitals.

Defoe tells us that the house was fatal to Dr Williams, the Bishop of Chichester, who on arriving to visit Lord Scarbrough 'was thrown out of his coach, or rather threw himself out, being frighted by the unruliness of his horses, and broke his leg in the fall, which, his lordship being in years, was mortal to him: he died in a few days after.'

The vaulted cellar.

9 'Adam's Name was Lumley'

RICHARD, THE SECOND Earl of Scarbrough, seems to have been an agreeable man. According to Hervey, he was 'bred in camp, and from thence brought to Court, and had all the gallantry of the one and the politeness of the other; he was amiable and beloved . . .' Educated at Eton and Cambridge, he became a fellow of King's College. He was Whig MP for East Grinstead from 1708 to 1710 and for Arundel from 1710 to 1715. Lieutenant-Colonel of the Queen's Regiment of Horse, he served against the Jacobites at the Battle of Preston in 1715. He was Lord of the Bedchamber to the Prince of Wales in 1714 and Master of the Horse to him from 1714 to 1727. He refused the offer of the post of Lord Lieutenant of Ireland in 1734. He was evidently in bad health from 1737 to 1739 and even thought to have become mad as a result of a blow on the head which he received after his carriage overturned. Eventually he committed suicide at his house in Grosvenor Square by shooting himself in the mouth with a pistol. This he is supposed to have done on the day before he was to marry Isabella, the widow of the second Duke of Manchester. According to Francis Hare, the then Bishop of Chichester, Lord Scarbrough was 'in great intimacy' with the Duchess.

From the various contemporary accounts of this tragedy it seems that the Earl, who was a most conscientious person, was greatly disturbed by the fact that a state secret which he unintentionally divulged to the Duchess was repeated by her to someone notoriously indiscreet. This, coupled with his accident, ill-health and other political worries, seems to have brought on the fit of depression which led to the disaster. Hervey described the second Earl as 'amiable and beloved' and 'fit to be trusted in the most important affairs'. His death was a terrible tragedy. He had evidently spent a good deal of time at Stansted. He knew Alexander Pope whose friend and patron, John Caryll, lived nearby at Harting. From a letter of Pope's which mentions a postponed visit to Stansted, it is known that he was resident in the house in 1727, and from a letter of Lord Scarbrough himself in the Newcastle Papers it is clear that he was there again in May 1734. But it appears that he was less interested in Stansted than in Lumley Castle where in 1721 he commissioned the playwright-architect, Sir John Vanbrugh, to carry out certain changes.

Thomas, the third Earl, was the next surviving brother and the fourth

The 2nd Earl of Scarbrough,
by Sir Godfrey Kneller, 1717.

son of the first Earl. He was born in 1691, and educated at Eton and
became a Captain in Colonel Tyrrell's Regiment of Dragoons and
Lieutenant-Colonel of Lord Hinchinbroke's Regiment of Foot and of
Ancaster's Regiment. He was Clerk to the Council of the Duchy of Lancaster from 1716 to 1731 and Envoy Extraordinary to Portugal from 1722
to 1725. His sumptuous entertainments in Lisbon are said to have brought
him into serious financial difficulties. His debts amounted at one time to
nearly £24,000 which included over £10,000 owing to his brother, the
second Earl. He was an anti-Walpole Whig and like his brother, James,
and his uncle, Henry Lumley, also MP for Arundel. It seems likely that
those members of the family who represented Arundel in Parliament made
reasonably regular visits to Stansted.

On the death of his unmarried cousin, James Saunderson, Earl of
Castleton, Thomas assumed the name of Saunderson and inherited his
estates in Yorkshire, including Sandbeck, where the present Earl of Scarbrough now lives. Although Thomas's son, Richard, the fourth Earl, no

doubt knew Stansted well, from the moment that the family acquired Sandbeck there seems to have been less interest in West Sussex. Thomas was a Knight of the Bath, Equerry to Frederick, Prince of Wales, and married a daughter of Field-Marshal the Earl of Orkney. Their son Richard, who succeeded him in 1752, was also a Whig and became Cofferer of the Household and later Deputy Earl Marshal. He married Barbara, the daughter of Sir George Savile.

However, the second Earl had not left his estates to the third Earl, but to their younger brother, James Lumley, who was MP for Chichester and later for Arundel as well as a Colonel in the Army. Jemmy, as he was known, was uncouth, notoriously illiterate, and made a fool of himself by prosecuting a lady who had horsewhipped him for refusing to pay her her winnings at whist. He died heavily in debt in 1766.

Jemmy left his Durham estates to his nephew, the fourth Earl of Scarbrough, and Stansted to George Montague-Dunk, second Earl of Halifax, another nephew, whose mother was Mary Lumley, the eldest daughter of Richard, first Earl of Scarbrough and sister of James Lumley who died in that year. Stansted thus remained with the Lumleys for almost exactly two hundred years. There are Lumley Mills near Emsworth, and the family arms are sculptured at Boxgrove. The family also had a town house, now called the Old Punch House, in Chichester. As Admiral Chambers suggests in his article in the *Sussex County Magazine*, the difficulties of Sussex country life and roads at the time must have been considerable. The Lumleys were accounted one of the oldest families in the kingdom. James I, on being told of the standing of his new subjects and perhaps bored with a lengthy dissertation of their antiquity, is said to have exclaimed: 'Oh mon! gang na further. I maun digest the knowledge I ha' this day gained, for I did na ken Adam's ither name was Lumley.' The family was indeed said to be descended from a Saxon noble, Liulph, who was a contemporary of William the Conqueror and whose statue is at Lumley Castle.

OPPOSITE *Lumley Seat today.*

10 'The Father of the Colonies'

THE EARL OF Halifax, who as will be seen from the above, was a first cousin of Richard, the fourth Earl of Scarbrough, was born in 1716. He married first Ann Dunk, only daughter of William Richards who had inherited in 1718 the property of Sir Thomas Dunk, 'a family of great clothiers' and had in consequence added the name 'Dunk'. It was a large fortune for those days – £110,000. The marriage with Lord Halifax did not take place until 1741, the wedding being delayed owing to the condition laid down in the will that the lady should only marry one who was engaged in commercial life. This obligation Halifax fulfilled by becoming a member of a London trading company. He thereafter added his wife's name to his family name of Montague. She died in 1735 when only twenty-eight years of age, and her husband, much to the surprise of the cynical wits of the period, seems to have shown real grief at her loss.

This Lord Halifax appears to have been one of those men, the product of their day, who could combine high living with a serious interest in public affairs. But the result of burning the candle at both ends seems to have

George Montague-Dunk, Earl of Halifax, in 1752.

The Entrance Hall, with various portraits, including Sir John Ponsonby, the founder of the family (above door).

been premature senility and early death. He possessed undoubted abilities but these were frittered away for lack of real force of character. He was said to have been unable to withstand the temptations which in those days beset men of birth and fortune.

At first he appears to have held several posts at the Court: Mastership of the Buckhounds, Lord of the Bedchamber and Chief Justiceship in Eyre of the Royal Parks and Forests south of the Trent. In politics he was a

Whig although a prominent opponent of Walpole. In 1744 he deserted
the Leicester party and joined the Pelham administration. He is said to
have spent £150,000 in fighting the borough of Northampton in opposition to Lord Northampton and Lord Spencer who were reputed to have
spent a quarter of a million between them. Lord Spencer was the father
of Georgiana, Duchess of Devonshire, and Henrietta Frances, Countess
of Bessborough, whose letters were edited by my father.

In 1748 Halifax became President of the Board of Trade where he
showed zeal in promoting the mercantile interests of the country. So much
was this the case that he has been described as 'the Father of the Colonies'.
The town of Halifax, Nova Scotia, was called after him. During this period
my own ancestor, William, second Earl of Bessborough, married Caroline,
daughter of the Duke of Devonshire. His eldest son, Frederick, married
Lord Spencer's daughter, Henrietta Frances. Portraits of all of them may
be seen at Stansted. William was a Lord of the Admiralty and a member
of the Board of the Treasury. He was succeeded at the Treasury in 1759
by Lord North, and himself became Postmaster-General. As they were
both Whigs and served in the same Governments, Bessborough must have
known Halifax well. I suspect he held no higher opinion of him than Lord
Spencer and others, and there is no evidence that any Ponsonbys,
Cavendishes or Spencers came to Stansted in Halifax's time.

After the accession of George III, Lord Halifax rejoined the Court. In
1761 he became Viceroy of Ireland and, in 1762, First Lord of the
Admiralty and a prominent member of Lord Bute's inner cabinet. He took
a leading part in the prosecution of Wilkes who was for the time forced
to flee the country, and the affair ended in Halifax being involved in heavy
damages. His reputation was failing when in 1763 Pitt was called upon
to form an administration and refused to have Halifax in any important
post 'as being in bad circumstances'. In 1766 he was one of the peers who
protested against the repeal of the Stamp Act. But his abilities were failing,
and we hear him described as 'the weakest but most amiable of the set'. In
1770 he was again in office though by this time (aged only fifty-four) already
suffering from senility. Horace Walpole had previously described him as
'honest and well disposed', and 'a man of moderate sense and great application, but warm, overbearing and ignorant of the world'. Now he could
only speak of him 'as being too old to learn and too sottish and too proud
to suspect what he wanted'. His profusion in building and planting and
also attentions to a favourite mistress seem to have made him poor and
impelled him to seek to recover himself by discreditable means. He
certainly got lost in the forest!

11 *A Singer from Drury Lane*

A YEAR OR two after Lady Halifax's death, the Earl happened to hear a
singer called Miss Faulkner, in reality Mrs William Donaldson, the adopted
daughter of a Dublin printer. According to *Records of . . . John Taylor* (1832)
he was 'so charmed by her musical powers that he actually fainted with
ecstasy'. Already well known from appearances at Covent Garden and
Marylebone Gardens, Mrs Donaldson became notorious as Lord Halifax's
mistress. She accompanied him to Ireland when he was Viceroy and
became well known as a place-monger – a way of raising money employed
by several notable men of the day. In 1770 her reminiscences were
published under what would seem to us today to be a proudly blatant
title: *The Genuine Memoirs of Miss Faulkner, otherwise Mrs. D*** L***n or
Countess of H****** in Expectancy*. These were no doubt written by her
publisher Mr William Bingley. In 1769 *The Town and Country Magazine*,
in the histories of their *têtes-à-têtes*, describes how 'Dunkaro' (Lord Halifax)
when a widower formed a connection with a married woman called

'Marianne' and 'Dunkaro' (Mrs Donaldson and Lord Halifax) in 1769.

51

'Marianne' (Mrs Donaldson), who was a popular success as Polly in the *Beggar's Opera* at Drury Lane. 'Never', says Mr Bingley, 'was any new performer so applauded.' According to the magazine 'Dunkaro's great passion for music induced him to yield his heart to Marianne.'

Marianne's husband was a customs official. To quote Eileen Harris writing in *Country Life*, 'Mr Donaldson was no more successful as a husband than he had been as a lover of the rival Irish actress, Miss Graham, or was later to be as the author of the novel, *The Life and Times of Bartholomew Sapskull*, 1768.' He was given lucrative employment in the West Indies and Mrs Donaldson's influence daily increased over Dunkaro. She was well considered by the servants and described as his lady.

Indeed she appears to have been a delightful character. She bore him two daughters as well as acting as governess to his legitimate children and teaching them music. It is related in her memoirs that she spent a good deal of time at Lord Halifax's country seat which was most probably Stansted. Finally one day he informed her that he was to be married to someone else. In a state of distraction this 'sweet-tempered' girl, as she is described in the memoirs, visited Lord Halifax and with her daughters gained entry to his London house, although the servants had been instructed to keep her out. She then persuaded him to break off his engagement. As a result the pair became, in the words of *The Town and Country Magazine*, 'the happiest toast . . . in the whole circle of gallantry and amorous connections'.

It was probably at the forceful insistence of Mrs Donaldson that Theodosius Keene – elder son of Henry Keene who designed the Radcliffe Observatory in Oxford – was employed to design Racton Tower, a folly that was half-way between a castle and a pagoda, with turrets at each point of its triangular plan. His only other known work is Maidenhead Town Hall. According to a letter to the publisher, signed 'Civis' and published at the end of *The Genuine Memoirs*, Mrs Henry Keene was one of the 'several ladies of easy virtue' who accompanied Lord Halifax's 'favourite Sultana' to Ireland, and secured for her husband (described as 'a contented cuckold' and 'first gentleman of the bedchamber to his Lordship') the surveyorship of Dublin Castle. For this Keene was paid £500 a year in England, 'without an obligation binding him to cross the herring-pond, to super-intend the duties of this nominal office'.

The Earl employed Henry Keene to design the tower of Westbourne Church in 1770. Theodosius Keene exhibited a drawing of Racton Tower under the title *A View of Stanstead Castle, near Emsworth* at the Society of Artists in 1772. But the rococo caprice of it was already old-fashioned, and only ten years later Walpoole found that, for elegance, the 'edifice'

LEFT *Henrietta Frances, Countess of Bessborough.*
RIGHT *Georgiana, Duchess of Devonshire –*
both by Angelica Kauffmann.

William, 2nd Earl of Bessborough, at the entrance to
Marylebone Fields, by Sir Peter Francis Bourgeois, 1798.

*Eighteenth-century pastels showing the east front of the old Wyatt House
(above) and the view of the north side with the Isle of Wight beyond
(below).*

was 'by no means proportionate to the prodigious expense which the raising of it cost his lordship'. The view from Stansted's west-facing dining
room, which would have been on the *piano nobile*, was itself so good that,
at Racton, a traveller feels himself in no very good humour after tediously
climbing up so many steps, and to such a height, to be rewarded for his
pains with nothing but disappointment'. 'Very ugly tower just built', was
Horace Walpole's comment in *Journals of Visits to Country Seats* (1770).

The Tower was reputed to have been the resort of ladies and gentlemen
of such ill-fame that Lord Halifax is said to have ordered its destruction.
This is a curious allegation for Lord Halifax died in 1771, yet the Tower
appears still to be intact in Grimm's drawing which is dated 1782, the
year after Richard Barwell purchased Stansted. The explanation may be
that Halifax only ordered the interior to be dismantled and the exterior
was left to fall into a ruin of its own accord. Or it may be that it was
the pious Lord Dartmouth who arranged for its partial demolition. As
will be seen below Lord Dartmouth was then the owner of Racton House
and farm. There seems no particular reason why the grandiose Indian
Nabob, Barwell, should have wished to see it destroyed.

The Tower is also said to have been used by smugglers to signal to ships
at sea. It certainly could have served as a landmark for ships entering
Chichester, Bosham, Emsworth and Langstone Harbours. As Presidents
of the Board of Trade neither Lord Halifax nor Lord Dartmouth would
have been well disposed to the smugglers, and this may have constituted
another reason for its destruction. At any rate it is now in ruins.

Racton is described in the Domesday Book as being part of the Earldom
of Roger de Montgomery. It was surveyed under the hundred of *Ghidentroi*
thus: *Ivo holds Rachitone of the Earl. Fulco held it of the Saxon monarch.* In the
latter part of the thirteenth century Hugh Sanzaver held the manor which
later became the property of Roger Gunter. His descendants (including
the Colonel Gunter who helped Charles II escape) enjoyed it until by marriage it passed in 1754 to William Legge, second Earl of Dartmouth.

During his five years at Stansted, Lord Halifax was intensely active in
improving the park. He built a charming Ionic temple, originally domed,
which he named Lumley Seat, in honour of his uncle's family. The main
rotunda of this temple was destroyed by a fire during the Second World
War but was restored by Ewen and Nicky Macpherson in 1966. The architect is not known, but it may have been Thomas Wright of Durham, who
worked extensively at Horton House, Northamptonshire, Lord Halifax's
principal seat. Wright, an astronomer and garden designer as well as an
architect, was something of an old friend, his talents having first been dis-

Racton Tower drawn by Grimm in 1782.

covered by Lord Scarbrough. He it was who built Hampton Court House
for Lord Halifax and Mrs Donaldson, a retreat conveniently near London
and adjacent to Bushy House, which Lord Halifax already occupied as
ranger to Bushy Park.

In addition to Lumley Seat and Racton Tower, Lord Halifax's work
at Stansted probably also included the curious column over the remains
of the present well-head at the south end of the arboretum, shown in a
beautiful series of late eighteenth-century pastel views, and began land-
scaping the Deer Park.

The house itself at this time, particularly as regards the pictures, is described by Walpole: 'Stanstead, Lord Halifax's, a better house, rather a
little older [than Uppark]. Fine carving by Gibbons over the chimney
of the Salon, particulary two Vases. Good whole length of Godomar when
old. Head of Sir Robert Cotton with frame by Gibbons. Beautiful small
Cuyp in Style of Wouwermans but still better, and the best I ever saw
of him; a brown horse, a white one & cocks & hens on the right. Its companion. Two larger, one a moonlight like Vandermeer, tother cows in a
storm of lightening. Famous picture of the Tribute money by Michael
Angelo Caravaggio, was his Uncle Halifax's and brought from Horton.
Garrick between Tragedy and Comedy [by Reynolds] cost £300. Com-

Racton Tower today.

edy, charming, Garrick quite farcical. Duke of Marlborough's tapestries. Most beautiful view from a new Temple, exactly like a Claud Lorrain.'

In the year before he died Lord Halifax offered parishioners of Westbourne Church the choice of an endowment for a Sunday afternoon sermon or a spire. The church dated, like Stansted, from the twelfth century and had for long been under the patronage of the Earls of Arundel. Faced with these alternatives the parishioners chose a spire because, they thought, it would always point to heaven whereas a sermon might not. The shingled spire was built of Stansted oak in 'Chinese taste' with an oaken balcony midway, but these ornamentations were unfortunately removed in 1860. These and other changes are recorded in the booklet on Westbourne Church by Lindsay Fleming.

It was no doubt thus that Lord Halifax, who died a few months later in 1771 and had been the owner of Stansted for only five years, came to leave it to his natural daughter, Anna Donaldson, who had meanwhile married Richard Archdell. But the family affairs were in such a state that soon after a brief visit of George III and Queen Charlotte in 1778 the trustees had no option but to put the estate on the market; and in 1781 it was sold to the Indian Nabob, Richard Barwell. It was then that the rectory of Westbourne was disposed of and it was no doubt at this time also that the 'gold and embroidered chairs' which were still there in Lewis Way's time were offered to Queen Charlotte, who nonetheless refrained from buying them because she found the price prohibitive.

12 *The Psalm-singing Earl*

LORD DARTMOUTH MARRIED the daughter of Sir Charles Gunter Nicholl and became a Fellow of the Society of Arts in the same year, 1754, as he came into Racton – that is to say while James Lumley was still the owner of Stansted and some twelve years before Lord Halifax inherited the place. I am including some references to Lord Dartmouth because, although he did not live at Stansted, the links between Stansted and Racton have always been close and were perhaps especially so during the eighteenth century when Lord Halifax built Racton Tower. The Gunters and the Legges lived in Racton House; and Halifax and Dartmouth, despite their very different characters, followed somewhat similar political careers. But Lord Dartmouth is the only personality I have ventured to describe who did not himself own Stansted. Racton remained in the Legge family until it was sold by the late Earl.

Although fifteen years his junior, Dartmouth must have been well known to Halifax; he too became President of the Board of Trade. This was in 1766 in Lord North's administration when Halifax was amongst those who were protesting against the repeal of the Stamp Act. He became Colonial Secretary in 1772 (a year after Halifax's death) and was Lord Privy Seal from 1775 to 1782. As a patron of the arts it seems possible that he may have influenced Halifax in the building of Racton Tower.

Benjamin Franklin, whose house in Craven Street in London my wife is arranging to restore, described Dartmouth as 'a truly good man who wished sincerely a good understanding with the Colonies but does not seem to have strength equal to his wishes'. In March 1775, Dartmouth recommended Lord North's conciliatory propositions to the Governors of the American colonies. In September of the same year he received the 'olive branch' from Richard Penn, but later intimated that no notice should be taken of it. In the following year he opposed the Duke of Grafton's proposal for conciliation with America, declaring that the only remedy was an overpowering force. However, as we now know, the forces were not overpowering; and in that sense Dartmouth found himself on the losing side.

There is no doubt that Dartmouth was an amiable and a pious man without a great deal of administrative capacity. George III, who may have seen him when he visited Stansted in 1778, was deeply attached to him:

Engraving of Stansted in 1789, from The European Magazine.

'How very dear he will always be to my heart.' That was the year in which the King refused to allow North to resign to receive Chatham as Chief Minister.

Lord Dartmouth himself had a strong attachment to the Methodists and acquired the nickname of 'The Psalm-singer'. Cowper alluded to him as 'one who wears a coronet and prays'. Dartmouth College in the United States was named in his honour, and he was evidently one of its most zealous promoters. Lord Dartmouth had eight sons, the eldest of whom succeeded him and held Government Office; the second became a barrister and Groom of the Bedchamber to the Prince of Wales; the third was a Lieutenant-Colonel; the fourth graduated from Christchurch but, like the second and third sons, died young. The remaining sons all lived longer, the fifth becoming Under-Secretary in the Irish Office, the sixth Admiral of the Blue, the seventh Bishop of Oxford and the eighth Archdeacon and Chancellor of Winchester. Lord Dartmouth sat for Sir Joshua Reynolds five times and the artist twice painted his wife.

As owner of Racton Lord Dartmouth may also have had an interest in Lordington or *Lordlington* which was a hamlet or tithing of Racton, and had for long been inhabited by the Pole family who were said to be descended from Cadwaladr, the mythical king of the Britains. Lordington later passed from the Poles to the Phipps Hornby's, who lived there as friendly neighbours. They were at Lordington Park while Lordington House is now occupied by Sir Michael Hamilton and his wife, the former Lavinia Ponsonby, like myself a direct descendant of Frederick, third Earl of Bessborough, and Henrietta Frances, daughter of the First Earl Spencer.

59

13 *The Indian Nabob*

RICHARD BARWELL, WHO bought Stansted from Lord Halifax's daughter in 1781, was very different from the Fitzalans, the Lumleys, the Montagues and the Legges. He spent the early part of his life in the service of the East India Company, was a friend of Warren Hastings, rose to be a member of the Supreme Council of Bengal and at the age of thirty-eight came home very rich. He had saved Warren Hastings from being outvoted on the Council, thus enabling him to carry out the policy which contributed much to the building up of British India. Hastings said that Barwell possessed 'much experience, a solid judgement, much greater fertility of resources than I have, and his manners are easy and pleasant'. But he may not have been a very likeable character; Sir Philip Francis, who was also on the Governor-General's Council and an opponent of Warren Hastings, was Barwell's sworn enemy and described him as 'cruel, cunning, rapacious, tyrannical and profligate'. Francis was the supposed author of the scandalous *Letters of Junius*. There was always a conflict between him and Barwell, which was usually waged over the card table, and on one occasion Barwell is said to have lost as much as £20,000.

Barwell's fortune was reputed to have been between £400,000 and £1,000,000 and not to have been obtained by straightforward means. General Clavering, who was also a member of the Council, and whose daughter's hand was sought by both Barwell and Francis, alleged misappropriation of funds; and the celebrated bloodless duel took place in which Clavering missed Barwell, who refrained from returning the General's fire. While in India he also gambled heavily with Philip Francis and laid himself open to pillory in a pamphlet entitled *The Intrigues of a Nabob; or Bengal the Fittest Soil for Lust* (1780) published by a wronged husband, Henry Thompson.

Barwell bought Stansted for a sum variously estimated as being between £90,000 and £192,500. William Hickey gives the lower figure and, as an alleged friend of Barwell (although only in his late teens when Barwell died), he may have known. The estate which Barwell bought extended far beyond Stansted and the neighbouring farms. It included land in the parishes of Westbourne, Racton, Stoughton, Compton, Up Marden, East Marden, Treyford, Chidham, Bosham and Apuldram. Barwell rebuilt the house regardless of expense.

According to Dallaway's *Western Division of Sussex*, Barwell employed James Wyatt and Joseph Bonomi (the latter, perhaps to make good the former's notorious inefficiency) in 1786–91. A few years earlier, Capability Brown had drawn 'many plans' for the house and also the grounds, according to his account books. He visited Stansted twice in 1781. Perhaps this was the time at which three magnificent avenues (only two of which remain today) were cut through the forest, and it may have been at Brown's behest that the clumps of beeches so much admired today were planted in the East Park. However, an estate map of 1785 suggests that little was done. Horace Walpole intimates that Brown was employed on both house and grounds at the time of his death in 1783, and that later Barwell called in James Wyatt and Joseph Bonomi to complete the job. The result, which must have been very much as portrayed in the print from the *European Magazine* and two pastels, sent Dallaway into raptures. He quotes Horace Walpole as seeing a resemblance in the landscapes of Claude Lorraine.

Wyatt and Bonomi encased the house in white brick and added double porticos, similar to those at Wyatt's nearby Goodwood House, to the east and west elevations. Each portico had sixteen Doric and Ionic columns, those on the west front being respectively $16\frac{1}{4}$ and $14\frac{1}{2}$ ft high. The old stables and offices, which had stood either side of the forecourt, were removed in favour of new pavilions, connected to the house by curving Doric colonnades 12 ft in breadth and open at the sides. Above each colonnade, a balustrade concealed lead cisterns. 'These,' wrote Dallaway, 'are supplied by a curious hydraulic machine, distant nine furlongs, and 199 feet below them. It throws up seven hog heads in an hour.'

Contemporaries thought the house much improved: 'The effect, from every point of view, is strikingly magnificent,' considered Dallaway, 'and nothing can exceed the gracefulness of the porticos, which give an air and character to the whole, peculiar to the most admired of the Italian villas in the neighbourhood of Rome and Florence.' But the alterations were less dramatic inside: 'Several of the very handsome apartments have undergone no change.' Among the pictures, Walpole noticed a Cuyp ('the best I ever saw of him') and *Garrick between Comedy and Tragedy*.

The house and park in Barwell's time can be seen in the series of pastels already mentioned. Although these show the park thronged with admiring passers-by, this was, initially, by no means the case. Barwell's young friend, William Hickey, writing in his *Memoirs*, recalled that he 'made it his study to render himself obnoxious to persons of all ranks, shutting up gates and paths through the park that had, as an indulgence, been always open to

The west front of the Wyatt House.

the public; His very name from such conduct was soon held in such detes-
tation that men, women and children hissed and hooted him as he passed
in all his oriental state through the villages.'

Although Barwell sought to rectify the bad impression by holding a typically lavish dinner for the neighbouring gentry, habits at Stansted
evidently remained the talk of the county. Wrote Lady Newdigate, a
frequent visitor, in one of her letters; 'The hours of ye family are what
ye Polite World wd not conform to, viz. Breakfast at $8\frac{1}{2}$, dine at $3\frac{1}{2}$, supper
at 9 and go to bed at 10, but everybody is at Liberty to order breakfast,
Dinner or supper into their own Rooms & no questions ask'd.'

George Augustus Walpoole, describing Stansted in 1782 in his *The New
British Traveller*, declared that:

The prospect from this seat is beautiful beyond description, especially from the
roof which is flat and covered with lead. . . . The interjacent country is beautifully
diversified with wood and water, cornfields and meadows and interspersed with
towns, villages and farms. To the eastward is a charming country decorated with
gentlemen's seats and rural habitations. Chichester spire is distinctly seen and
adds greatly to the beauty of the perspective. The park is embellished with two
buildings, both erected by the late Earl, one is a temple called Lumley Seat, raised
in grateful memory of the donor, it consists of a handsome saloon ornamented
with paintings well executed, in front is a portico which carries the view across
the park quite to the sea. The other building is a triangular tower or gazebo,
consisting of several stories and crowned at the top wtih a flag-staff; from the
leads of the upper story the eye takes in an unbounded prospect over that part
of Sussex which lies between the Downs and the coast to the east and south, and
beyond the Isle of Wight to the westward, having a clear view of the British Channel in an uninterrupted line from point to point.

The south front of the Wyatt House,
with Lumley Seat on the right.

But as we have already heard, the panorama did not blind Walpoole to the extravagance of the building, and he goes on to grumble that the view was no compensation for the long climb up to the top of the tower. Returning to the house, his description of the pictures complements that previously given:

The house . . . contains a very excellent collection of pictures, some of which have been executed by masterly hands, particularly one of our Saviour after his resurrection showing Himself to His doubting disciples. Another, much admired, done by the famous blacksmith of Antwerp; several beautiful landscapes, fruit pieces, and portraits; among the latter Van Trump and Bondamar the Spanish Ambassador, esteemed striking likenesses; nor ought the elegant picture done by Sir Joshua Reynolds, the subject 'Comedy and Tragedy contending for the Possession of Garrick', to pass unnoticed. In the upper appartments are some beautiful tapestry-hangings representing different military scenes in Flanders during the victorious Duke of Marlborough's campaigns. The soil on which this house stands is so remarkably dry that none of these paintings or the furniture of the apartments are ever affected by damps, nor are fires necessary in the winter to preserve them from it. It may, therefore, be concluded that few situations can be more eligible for health.

Elizabeth Iremonger, the daughter of Joshua Iremonger of Wherwell

Priory in Hampshire, writing on 24 July 1785, to her friend, Miss Heber, said that she had recently been staying at Uppark with her aunt, Sarah Lethieullier, who was then married to Matthew Fetherstonhaugh, but that they had had to vacate their places to the Prince of Wales (afterwards George IV) and his party. While she was there a marriage took place nearby which, she says, surprised most people:

Mr Barwell, the great East Indian of Stansted, to Miss Coffin, a very pretty little Girl not 16, of American extraction. Till a fortnight before this Event He kept a very Beautiful Mistress close to this Park, by whom he has several Children, and till very lately He declared most strongly against Matrimony. He seems a good-natured man, but the Mogul prevales strongly, I think, in his way of Life and Conversation. Mrs Barwell is in possession of a most Noble Park and immense Riches: I hope she will be able to maintain her Influence over Him.

Then again on 19 August 1786, Miss Iremonger writes from Uppark that she had, six weeks previously, been to a ball given by Mr Barwell:

Next Monday we are invited to another & we think it an odd manœuvre that the Gentlemen are all invited to Dinner, and all the female part of the families to spend the evening. It is a charming House for these gay purposes, & every thing was very well conducted the last time.

Barwell was MP for Winchelsea in 1790. He is supposed, on being called upon to give information on a certain Indian inquiry by a Committee of the House of Commons, to have refused to attend the summons and to have pretended to be absent from his house when messengers were sent to enforce attendance. Ultimately he was brought before them under threat of force and received a severe rebuke from the Chairman. This was all the more galling in that it was delivered by another Anglo-Indian General who had been a former antagonist and junior in Calcutta.

Barwell's daring in treating a Committee of the House of Commons with contumely brought disgrace upon him. The event was considered the more extraordinary in that he presumed so to act when he was himself a candidate for the House he was thus indecently insulting. Never, says Hickey, was a purse-proud and haughty man so mortified as Barwell on this occasion. Barwell died at Stansted in 1804 and an impressive monument by Nollekens, with a highly eulogistic inscription, was erected in his memory in Westbourne parish church. Barwell's trustees sold the Stansted estate for £173,000 to Lewis Way. There are various statements as to precisely what Way bought; but the detailed plan and valuation made for Barwell in 1785 give the acreage as about 5,500.

ABOVE *Richard Barwell, from a portrait by Sir Joshua Reynolds.*
RIGHT *The Nollekens monument to Barwell in Westbourne Church.*

THIS MONUMENT
IS DEDICATED TO THE MEMORY
OF RICHARD BARWELL, ESQ^{RE}
OF STANSTEAD PARK IN THE COUNTY OF SUSSEX;
WHO IN THE SERVICE OF THE HON^{BLE} EAST-INDIA COMPANY,
DURING A PERIOD OF TWENTY-THREE YEARS,
ATTAINED TO SUCH SITUATIONS OF HIGH TRUST AND EMOLUMENT,
AS HIS TALENTS AND UNBLEMISHED REPUTATION
MOST JUSTLY ENTITLED HIM.
WITH AN UNDERSTANDING STRONG AND CULTIVATED,
AND A MIND OPEN AND HONOURABLE,
WERE UNITED OTHER QUALITIES RARE AND ESTIMABLE;
AND BY ALL WHO COULD APPRECIATE
AFFECTION TOWARDS HIS FAMILY, ATTACHMENT TO HIS FRIENDS,
AND BENEVOLENCE WIDELY SPREAD AROUND,
HE WAS RESPECTED WHEN LIVING,
AND DIED LAMENTED, ON THE SECOND DAY
OF SEPTEMBER, 1804,
IN THE SIXTY-SECOND YEAR OF HIS AGE.

Nollekens F.

14 Lewis Way

LEWIS WAY WAS another curious character. He was the second son of Squire Benjamin Way, the owner of Denham Place, Buckinghamshire. He was born in London in 1772, and educated at Eton and Merton College, Oxford, where he had a distinguished career. The teaching of his early years was strongly evangelical, but against the limitations of his life at Denham weighed the influence of Eton and Oxford. He earnestly desired to go into the Church, but his father insisted on his becoming a barrister. One day, when seated in his chambers, he was visited by a dapper old gentleman of the name of John Way, who announced that he wished to make the acquaintance of Lewis because they bore the same surname although in fact they were not related. The old man had been the agent of the Earl of Mansfield and by thrift and business ability accumulated a large fortune. He had intended to leave his fortune to his heir, Thomas Way, but when, on inviting him to dine, Thomas drew from his pocket a corkscrew to open an obdurate bottle of port, John Way came to the conclusion that any man who went about with a corkscrew in his pocket was unlikely to make good use of his wealth. It was thus that he turned to Lewis Way, made him his protégé and, when he died in 1804, left him some £300,000.

John Way had intended to found a religious institution with his wealth but relegated the task to his successor. The purchase of Stansted by Lewis Way was not only to provide a home for his wife and children but eventually to utilise it for a charitable institution under his own supervision. His first act at Stansted was to build a chancel to what became his private chapel and to replace the Tudor by Regency Gothic windows. After a period of indecision and unrest lasting six years, Way made up his mind under rather unusual circumstances. He decided that his life's work was to be the conversion of the Jews to Christianity and their restoration to Palestine. So he determined to found a Hebrew College at Stansted which then became the haunt of a medley of guests, men of high principle vying with rogues for his friendship. Sixteen young Jews, who were guests in the house, heard the false but distressing rumour that Way was bankrupt. The young converts immediately decamped taking with them every object on which they could lay hold including the silver spoons of their host. It was this episode that prompted Macaulay to write the verse:

*Miniatures of Mr and Mrs Lewis Way (1769
and 1768) by John Smart.*

Each, says the proverb, to his taste. 'Tis true,
Marsh loves a controversy, Coates a play,
Bennet a felon, Lewis Way a Jew,
The Jew, the silver spoons of Lewis Way.

In 1815, after the Battle of Waterloo, the Holy Alliance was formed
in Europe. The Emperors of Russia and Austria and the Kings of Prussia
signed a manifesto declaring that their conduct should be regulated by
the principles of the Christian religion. This gave Lewis Way an idea. He
thought that some clause should be introduced into the Protocol securing
for the Jews the privilege of purchasing land in Palestine. With this was
interwoven the object which he had at heart: their conversion to
Christianity. He decided to visit Tsar Alexander I to plead his cause.

First of all, in order to further his object, he was ordained priest in 1817.
He then applied to his uncle, Edward Cooke, who was Under-Secretary
for Foreign Affairs, for a letter of introduction to the Emperor. With some
reluctance Cooke, who was a frequent visitor to Stansted and frankly
deplored Way's 'visionary flightiness', eventually submitted and arrange-
ments were made for the meeting. After crossing Europe the momentous
interview took place in Moscow in January 1818. The autocrat of all the
Russias and his new acquaintance from Stansted were, it is said, much
attracted to each other, and three further long interviews took place.

Drawn & Engraved by I. Higham for the Excursions through Sussex

STANSTED HOUSE,

The Seat of the Rev.ᵈ Lewis Way,

SUSSEX.

The east front, from a print of 1820.

Finally the Emperor charged Lewis Way to go to the Congress which was to be held the following autumn at Aix-le-Chapelle in order to plead his cause personally. On leaving Moscow Way indited a long panegyrical poem to Tsar Alexander. He wrote it 'on a bitter night in an open sledge' but even his conscientious biographer, Mrs Stirling, found the ode too long to quote in full.

15 *The Wandering Jew*

WHEN THE TIME came Lewis Way hobnobbed at Aix with his Imperial friend and finally addressed the assembled crowned heads and plenipotentiaries, who included Metternich, Richelieu, Castlereagh, Wellington and Nesselrode. His eloquence persuaded them to add a clause to the Protocol promising tolerance to the Jews and their entry into the family of society. Then the Tsar and Way bade each other a sad farewell. They never met again. Nor did anything come of his sensational appeal on behalf of the Jews.

Lewis Way, who had by now nicknamed himself 'the Wandering Jew', reached Stansted in time to spend Christmas with his family. A few weeks later, in January 1819, took place the consecration of the Chapel which he had enlarged and decorated and which, as will be seen below, inspired the poet John Keats to write some of his finest verse. Way himself preached at Stansted and solemnly dedicated the house and the estate to God to be used as a college for the training of Jews and foreign missionaries. He petitioned Lord Liverpool for a charter for this purpose but was not successful in obtaining his desire.

Lewis Way did a good deal of replanting of the forest while he was at Stansted. On one occasion he is reported as planning a new vista – probably the rough avenue which runs north-west from the house. Then, according to the plaque on the west wall of the Middle Lodge, 'the new plantation of this avenue' – presumably the main one – 'was commenced on the last day of the reign of King George III', that is to say in the year 1820. The plaque is surmounted by a crown with seven stars on its seven points and underneath's Way's inscription: *Corruptibilem pro incorruptibili*.

Among the habitués at Stansted at this time were Sir Benjamin West, President of the Royal Academy. Born of Quaker parents in Philadelphia, he was much employed by George III and painted the famous picture of the death of Wolfe. West's successor, Sir Thomas Lawrence, was also a frequent visitor. Way had no doubt met him at Aix-la-Chapelle when he was painting the assembled Sovereigns there. According to Way's daughter, Drusilla, the studios of both painters were frequently visited by the Ways in London. When they came to Stansted they were both regaled by hymn tunes played by Mrs Way on the organ – 'it had all black keys, no white' – which stood at the foot of the grand staircase. William Wilberforce, the philanthropist, was also well known at Stansted. His son, Samuel, the future bishop, preached his first sermon in the Chapel there. William no doubt returned to Stansted after the passing of his Bill for the abolition of slavery and again when he became Member of Parliament for Bramber not many miles away.

In 1822 the scheme for transforming Stansted into a college not having matured, and being considerably impoverished by his generosity, Lewis Way decided to let the house and winter abroad with his family. He went to Nice and was so struck by the poverty there that he started the *Promenade des Anglais* in order to give employment. His philanthropy soon earned him the soubriquet *Louis d'Or*. He continued his travels through Italy and then by ship to the Levant where he had long discussions with the eccentric traveller, Lady Hester Stanhope. While in Syria he fell ill and was unable to go on his pilgrimage to Jerusalem.

However in 1824 he was well enough to return to Paris. He purchased the Hotel Marbœuf there, transformed the adjoining hall into a chapel, took up his abode in the Hotel and acted as Chaplain in the Chapel. Two years later he and his family came to England and spent some time at Stansted. Once more Way tried to make Stansted into a College. Once more he failed to obtain a Charter. He therefore decided to sell the property and returned with his family to Paris. The English flocked to hear him preach, but his health was failing, and the Jews were still far from their promised land. In 1830 he and his family went to reside permanently at Leamington while continuing to finance the English Church in Paris. By this time his enthusiasm, his faith in human nature, besides his health and fortune had left him. He became haunted by a sense of futility and in 1840 he died.

————

OPPOSITE *The Tudor south front of the Chapel.*

70

16 *Drusilla's Memories*

YEARS LATER WHEN Way's daughter, Drusilla, was an elderly lady she wrote, according to Mrs Stirling, a few dim recollections of her childhood at Stansted and its bygone glories, of her brother, Albert, curled upon the deep oak window-sill of the Blue Room with a pile of encyclopaedias around him, of his collection of tiny chalk fossils in paper trays in his dark dressing-room and his insects and butterflies impaled on pins which were all connected by the children with Noah and his flood. There were 'the great tapestry drawing rooms, the wainscotted saloon, the oak room with its fine panelling, the great porticos, the cellar like a church, the oak chairs and tables with the Halifax acorns on them, the firedogs bearing the same design and the old organ with the black keys'.

'Not easy for you to follow', she wrote, 'tho' so graphic to me. The present dining room was, with us, the State bedroom given to Number One guests, like Mr Wilberforce or Bishop Ryder etc., because it was on ye ground floor, handy and comfortable. Over it was Queen Elizabeth's room with her picture. In its then North dressing-room the Downman pictures were taken. The front bedroom against this was called "the best room" because the furniture was more modern.' In that room was born their cousin, Mary Johnstone, who later married Sir Robert Buxton, the third Baronet of Shadwell Court, Norfolk.

Drusilla also tells us how one day the Duke of Clarence, afterwards William IV, who was staying at Lord Keith's at Purbrook, visited Stansted and how interested he was 'in the tapestries which Queen Anne had given to Lord Halifax [sic] which he said represented the Duke of Marlborough's wars'. The Duke of Clarence explained the tapestries to Drusilla's mother 'who ye figures were, etc.; and seemed quite at home with it, we two small ones following close, listening'. But there was a slight *contretemps* which annoyed Mrs Way. 'Unaware till the last moment', says Mrs Stirling, 'that the Duke was coming to luncheon Mrs Way hurriedly got together as suitable a repast for her Royal visitor as was practicable at a short notice. In those days all the food was placed upon the table, and, to fill up a gap, she ordered a "Resurrection Pie", a homely dish composed of promis-

---

OPPOSITE *The interior of the Chapel.*

73

Drusilla, Albert, Anna and Olivia,
the children of Lewis Way, by John
Downman, 1817.

cuous fragments, which was intended merely to swell the number of dishes
on the board, but otherwise to be ignored. What was her annoyance when
the young Prince, rejecting all the delicacies which were respectfully pres-
sed upon him, fixed upon the Resurrection Pie designed as a stop-gap,
and insisted upon partaking of this and no other!' This seems to have been
the last occasion on which members of the Royal Family visited Stansted
until, as will be seen below, Queen Elizabeth the Queen Mother, and the
Princess Royal, came to stay in my father's time.

There is such a wealth of information about Lewis Way, his family,
their curious friends and their various travels that I must be excused for
only touching a few highlights and concentrating mainly on their life at
Stansted. Those who are interested in reading full accounts of his interviews with the Tsar, with the other crowned heads of Europe and with
Pope Pius VII (the famous Gregorio Chiaramonti who defied Napoleon)
should consult A.M.W. Stirling's *The Ways of Yesterday*. Likewise those
who wish to delve into Lewis Way's extraordinary relations with Dr Joseph
Woolff and Lady Hester Stanhope and their discussions on the coming
of the millenium should read Lady Hester's own memoirs as well as Mrs
Stirling's book.

17 *The Chapel and John Keats*

THE CHAPEL WHICH Lewis Way restored and consecrated at Stansted is perhaps the most interesting of the buildings as they now stand. It lies apart from the present house, and would appear, both from its construction and from the eighteenth-century prints of the estate as laid out by Lord Scarbrough, to be part of the 1480 building which has already been discussed. Its main shell is good fifteenth-century brick although parts of the north-east walls in flint and stone appear to be of a much earlier date. It is doubtful whether it was originally a religious building. Certainly it had no proper foundations until Goodhart-Rendel's restoration in 1926. There is no indication of a chapel being among the buildings erected for Henry II in 1180 nor for Lord Mautravers three hundred years later, but

John Keats by William Hilton, after a miniature by Joseph Severn.

75

there is mention of a chapel in the survey of 1327. On the outside of his chapel, Way added little towers and battlements to the west front and curious sham Gothic pinnacles on the south face. He also covered the early brick with stucco which has since been removed. The windows were altered to Regency Gothic, and a plaster ceiling and ribs with appropriate and rather delicate embellishments of the same period make the nave distinctly attractive.

Who undertook this work for Lewis Way is not known. Goodhart-Rendel considered that the design of the plaster vaulting and the slender columns supporting it in the chancel seem 'far beyond the reach of the clever carpenters to whom much early Nineteenth Century Gothic is due, and the designer of them must have been exceptionally experienced and skilled in his art'.

The sanctuary has a canopy supported by wooden pillars and is most unusual for 1812. The painted east window is probably unique in being the only window in a Christian place of worship which is wholly Jewish in design and symbolism. There are inscriptions in Greek and Hebrew, embodying Way's aspirations for the conversion of Israel, and a beautiful eagle lectern of a design uncommon for the early nineteenth century.

Here we can make an attribution as to the artist: similar symbolism is incorporated in the chapel of Way's previous house, Denham Place, and this is signed by James Pearson, who was presumably responsible for the Stansted glass.

Goodhart-Rendel's restoration of the sanctuary with altar and reredos of his own design forms a gorgeous contrast to the simplicity of the nave. The object of Goodhart-Rendel's decoration and additional furnishing was to enhance the character of the building; the style of the new organ case, credence table and altar-gradine being closely assimilated to that of their surroundings.

The features of the windows in the Chapel have led to an important literary discovery. Among the personalities present at the consecration service was the poet John Keats. Towards the end of January 1819, Keats was staying in Chichester and later in Bedhampton and is known to have been at work on *The Eve of St Agnes* and *The Eve of St Mark*. While at Bedhampton he no doubt read in *The Hampshire Telegraph and Sussex Chronicle* the announcement that the Chapel was to be consecrated on the 25th day of January, the Feast of the Conversion of St Paul.

'I will not harm her, by the great St Paul', wrote Keats in the first line of stanza XVII in all manuscripts of *The Eve of St Agnes*. 'Tomorrow', wrote Brown, who was with Keats that Sunday, 'we shall go to Stanstead [sic]

The entrance to the Chapel, with Lewis Way's font
for total immersion.

to see Mr Way's Chapel consecrated by the two Bigwigs of Gloucester and St David's'.

This visit of Keats to Stansted is discussed in Robert Gittings' *John Keats: The Living Year*. The poet's decision to attend the service was, as Mr Gittings observes, momentous. It was a curious expedition for Keats to make, for he had an almost obsessive loathing of the clergy themselves and of religious ceremonies. He and Brown drove over from Bedhampton and arrived late to find the little Chapel crammed to the doors with three times as many people as it would normally hold. The service was very long and must have lasted from eleven o'clock to a late dinner time. Keats, the anti-clerical, described the expedition as follows in his letter of 24 February to George and Georgiana Keats:

The only time I went out from Bedhampton was to see a chapel consecrated – Brown, I, and John Snook the boy, went in a chaise behind a leaden horse. Brown drove, but the horse did not mind him. This chapel is built by a Mr Way, a great Jew converter, who in that line has spent one hundred thousand pounds.

He maintains a great number of poor Jews – *Of course his communion plate was stolen.* He spoke to the clerk about it. The clerk said he was very sorry, adding, '*I dare shay, your honour, it's among ush.*' The chapel is built in Mr Way's park. The consecration was not amusing. There were numbers of carriages – and his house crammed with clergy. They sanctified the chapel, and it being a wet day, consecrated the burial-ground through the vestry window. I begin to hate parsons; they did not make me love them that day, when I saw them in their proper colours. A parson is a Lamb in a drawing-room, and a Lion in a vestry.

The service was conducted by Bishop Ryder of Gloucester and Bishop Burgess of St David's, two of the leading churchmen of the age. Keats may have allowed his attention to wander but his eyes were watchful.

The coloured glass of the window in the north-west corner of the north side of the Chapel was 'embellished with the arms and cognizances of the Fitzalans', and it is hardly fanciful to suppose that Keats saw in these armorial bearings the source of two stanzas of *The Eve of St Agnes* for they contain an almost exact description of the window opposite which Keats spent two or three hours. The arms of the Montgomery, d'Aubigny and Fitzalan Earls of Arundel contained 'azure a lion rampant and a border or', and 'gules a lion rampant or'. Keats must have seen them on the diamond-shaped panes in the three arches of the window opposite him; and in the middle of each arch is the 'shielded scutcheon' through which, Robert Gittings suggests, an intermittent ray of sunlight may have fallen on the pectoral cross of one of the Bishops. Whether the Bishops at that time wore pectoral crosses is a matter of doubt. In any case that night at Bedhampton it seems that Keats wrote his first attempt at the famous stanzas XXIV and XXV:

> A Casement tripple arch'd and diamonded
> With many coloured glass fronted the Moon
> In midst w(h)ereof a shi(e)ld scutcheon shed
> High blushing gules; and she kneeled saintly down
> And inly prayed for grace and heavenly boon;
> The blood red gules fell on her silver cross
> And her white hands devout.

The glass of these northern windows was unfortunately blown out during the Second World War but has now been replaced. It is curious that armorial bearings of my own family placed on the south side by my father create a somewhat similar effect:

> Rose-bloom fell on her hands, together prest,
> And on her silver cross soft amethyst.

18 *The Eve of St Mark*

IT IS IN respect of *The Eve of St Mark* that Robert Gittings directs our attention to the east window in the Chapel. The idea that this window was the inspiration for the later poem belongs to Mrs J.R.H. Moorman, the daughter of Dr G.M. Trevelyan. Mr Gittings considers that this is especially clear in the second stanza of the poem, but I would suggest that the first may also derive its inspiration from the poet's visit to the Chapel at the time of the service of consecration.

> Each arched porch, and entry low,
> Was fill'd with patient folk and slow,
> With whispers hush, and shuffling feet,
> While play'd the organ loud and sweet.

*The Gothick north front of the Chapel,
as restored by Lewis Way.*

Is it pure chance that the arched porch and west entry at Stansted are especially low and that Stansted was the place where he had recently attended a religious service before writing these lines? In the second stanza Gittings observes that Keats introduced his heroine poring over an illuminated manuscript and maintains that the journey to Stansted asserted itself directly Bertha opened her book. This book, he says, has been called 'a quite impossible invention jumbling fantastically together things that could never have figured in the same manuscript': stars, angels' wings, martyrs in a fiery blaze, saints, silver rays, Moses' breastplate, a seven-branched candlestick, the covenantal Ark, the Lion of St Mark, cherubim – and golden mice.

Yet what might be impossible in a manuscript was not, as Gittings says, too fantastic for the mind of Lewis Way. And it is evidently to Keats' vigil in Stansted chapel that he owed the ingredients of the book. As we have said his nearest sight of the nave would have been the stained glass of the north-west window; but at a farther distance he would have seen the set of glass in the chancel; these were the east windows containing seven lights. At the head of each of these lights is a silver star and a small-winged cherub; the two northern lights are occupied by a seven-branched candlestick. In the three middle lights below the stars and cherubs, there is a rainbow and silver rays of light descending through golden clouds. Beneath is a fire in a brazier and the Ark of the Covenant with long-winged cherubim at each end; lying on some steps below this is the blossoming rod of Aaron. The two southern lights, though possibly invisible from where Keats stood, contain a table of brass or gold on which are piled the Tables of the Law together with a burning lamp. Finally, as Goodhart-Rendel observes, there was above the altar the marble book which was later moved to the west end and had its pages carved with names by way of a war memorial. Every part of this was, according to his daughter, Way's design – 'The idea throughout is the Gospel Dispensation, shadowed forth in that of the Law, or Moses a schoolmaster leading to Christ.'

The breastplate may, as Gittings says, have come into his head from the first lesson of the day, the fifth chapter of the Book of Wisdom, verse 18, which Keats had heard read by Way's curate: 'He shall put on

---

OPPOSITE *The chancel of the Chapel showing the Jewish imagery and Goodhart-Rendel's restorations, including the high altar which covers the original by Lewis Way.*

righteousness as a breastplate, and true judgement instead of an helmet.'

Mr Gittings regrets that we have no record of Bishop Burgess's sermon, for, as he says, it is possible that there might be found in it the golden mice, which, according to I Samuel, vi. 4, were inside the Ark. This was an unlikely piece of knowledge for Keats unless he had heard it recently expounded. 'This deliberate transcription of windows into a book is typical of Keats' way of work', says Mr Gittings. 'His imagination, all through his poetic life, was excited by paintings and pictorial images. The unique series of pictures in Way's glass naturally stimulated his imagination. In memory their dull gold, silver, flame and azure became the colouring of a medieval manuscript. The jumble of subjects is explained by the one place in England where such a collection could be seen, as it still can today, in Stansted Chapel.'

The day of the consecration was stormy, and no doubt after the service Keats went to Stansted House. As the front door was opened I have little doubt that as in stanza XL of *The Eve of St Agnes*

> The arras, rich with horsemen, hawk, and hound,
> Flutter'd in the beseiging wind's uproar;

(the tapestries dating from the Scarbrough's time) and that

> . . . the long carpets rose along the gusty floor. . .

as they do today whenever there is a south-west wind. Once in the house perhaps Keats partook of the feast which inspired him that night to write:

> Of candied apple, quince, and plum, and gourd;
> With jellies soother than the creamy curd,
> And lucent syrops, tinct with cinnamon;
> Manna and dates, in argosy transferr'd
> From Fez; and spicèd dainties, every one,
> From silken Samarcand to cedar'd Lebanon.

The *Hampshire Telegraph & Post* did in fact describe the feast as sumptuous, and so Keats wrote:

> These delicates he heap'd with glowing hand
> On golden dishes and in baskets bright
> Of wreathèd silver: sumptuous they stand
> In the retired quiet of the night.

At the end of his chapter on *The Eve of St Agnes* Mr Gittings concludes that 'quiet, in his own candlelit upper room at the mill-house (in Bed-hampton), Keats worked with an intensity only to be guessed at by the sight of his much-scored manuscript. While the wind, swirling up the estuary, rattled the dark window-pane, he completed one of the world's greatest narrative poems.' But he must also have had in mind some first thoughts for *The Eve of St Mark*.

In his foreword to the pamphlet on the Chapel by my father, the late Dr George Bell, Bishop of Chichester, declares that Stansted Chapel has a character of its own as a place of worship and that its beauty and charm are well known alike to the members of the family and to parishioners who attend the services Sunday by Sunday. He explains the origin of the Jewish features in the east window and elsewhere and refers to the peculiar fascination of the association with John Keats and the 'thousand things' which so perplexed Bertha in *The Eve of St Mark*:

> The stars of heaven, and angels' wings,
> Martyrs in a fiery blaze,
> Azure saints in silver rays,
> Moses' breastplate, and the seven
> Candlesticks John saw in heaven,
> The wingèd Lion of Saint Mark,
> And the Covenantal Ark,
> With its many mysteries . . .

One hundred and thirty years later, Father Neate, the incumbent of St George's Church in Paris, told me, while I was a Secretary at the British Embassy, that he had discovered in his Church silver Communion plate which was not used. The cup had the inscription 'Lewis Way, Stanstead Park' on the base. Did I not live at Stansted and who was Lewis Way? I told Father Neate the story and explained that this plate must have been left by Way in the Marbœuf church which he founded and been transferred to St George's when the Marbœuf church was destroyed by fire. The plate was then, through my wife, returned to the Chapel at Stansted where it had been used so frequently in the past and where it is now brought out on special feast days.

Many interesting and indeed fascinating sermons have been preached in the chapel. Two of them, one by Dr E. W. Kemp, the present Bishop of Chichester, at the dedication of the Banner of the European Parliament on 27 April 1975, and the other by the Reverend Canon R. T. Greenacre, Chancellor of Chichester Cathedral, on 25 January 1981 on the occasion of the Patronal Festival of the Conversion of St Paul, in which new light is shed on the character of Lewis Way, are given in Appendix IV. Like Father Neate, Canon Greenacre was also a former chaplain of the church which Way founded in Paris in 1824.

19 *Charles Dixon and the Wilders*

IN 1826 LEWIS WAY's executors sold Stansted to Charles Dixon, a wine merchant of London. I have been able to discover little about Dixon except that he was much revered in the neighbourhood for his philanthropy. In his obituary notice the *Hampshire Telegraph & Post* declared that he 'had earned a character and reputation for philanthropy and benevolence of the most extended nature'. Great indeed was the loss which 'almost every institution in Portsmouth and the neighbourhood' had suffered by his decease. There was hardly a charitable institution in the locality which had not benefited by his munificence. Portsmouth hospitals, schools for orphans and the poor, and seamen's homes were all deeply indebted to him. The neighbourhood was 'crowded with memorials to his piety' and that of his wife. Among them were Forestside Church which he built and Stansted College in Rowlands Castle which he founded for the benefit of 'six decayed merchants' who were 'members of the Church of England'. This curious College, now demolished, was administered by a Board of Trustees of whom the owner of Stansted was Chairman.

Charles Dixon died in 1855 aged eight-four. He appears to have been the first person to have been buried in the Chapel at Stansted. At any rate there is no evidence of any earlier grave inside or outside in the church-yard. Dixon's widow, Augustina Ivers Mary, then inherited the house. She had been previously married to a man named George Wilder by whom she had a son George who was a Captain in the Royal Horse Artillery. The son died in 1856 at the age of thirty-six and is also buried in the Chapel.

In 1865 the poet Henry Knight published an exquisitely slim volume entitled, *Leaves of Autumn from the Vale of Ems*, which he dedicated 'to Mrs Dixon of Stansted House, Sussex.' It included the following verses:

> Above those woods of ancient beech,
> Now reddening in the blaze
> Of sunset – far as eye can reach,
> See yon fair mansion raise
> Its head; while bids the day farewell,
> And gently comes the eve,
> In each bright closing flower-bell
> Its diamond drops to leave;

Charles Dixon, who purchased
Stansted in 1826.

While round it, to the whispering gales,
    In many a perfumed grove,
Pour the melodious nightingales
    Their dulcet songs of love;
And, silent glimmering in the sky,
    The star of eve appears,
As lovely as the soft blue eye
    Of a maiden dimmed with tears.

Ah, Stansted! many a grateful tear
    Has round thy walls been shed,
And floods of sorrow wet the bier
    Of him who's with the dead;
Too soon thy master passed away,
    Death closed that bounteous hand,
But green he'll live in memory
    Through all the mourning land;
Widows and orphans blessed his name,
    Lean hunger shunned his eye;
And he has won that deathless fame
    That lives beyond the sky.

It was Charles Dixon who employed Thomas Hopper to pull down the Wyatt and Bonomi's pavilions, and to erect the present stables and offices – the third set in the life of the house. Hopper had made his name by designing a Gothick conservatory in the style of Henry VII's chapel, but built of cast iron, at Carlton House, for the Prince Regent. This gave him

Cricket match at Stansted, by W. Pink, 1874.

a fashionable country-house practice, during which he remodelled Purley Hall, Berkshire, for John Wilder – a relation of Mrs Dixon's first husband, George Wilder. According to Dr Howard Colvin's *A Biographical Dictionary of British Architects*, it is said he refused a knighthood, as well as offers from the Tsar of Russia and the Duchess of Oldenburg to settle in St Petersburg.

Although he could, and would, design in any style, the work at Stansted was in his imposing but heavy Classical manner, which showed a preference for columnar attachments. The Stable wing consists of a pedimented, seven-bay central block, surmounted by a many-columned, rectilinear cupola. To either side are entrances based on the triumphal-arch motif, with pairs of Tuscan rather than Doric columns. Hopper may also have built the three lodges.

Mrs Dixon, who lived on until 1871 continuing the good works of her second husband, devised the estate in trust for the benefit of her grandson, George Wilder, who was then only six years old. This George eventually married Mary Laura O'Callaghan whose family lived at Deerleap in Rowlands Castle. He was twenty-one and she twenty-two. The family home was at Purley Hall in Surrey, but George and Mary lived on at Stansted in fine style until he died in 1896 at the age of forty-six as a result of pneumonia contracted on return from a yachting trip in which he had encountered especially stormy weather. She lived on until 1942 when she died at the age of ninety-two.

George and Mary were a devoted couple who loved the open air and many sports. Their twenty-five years of young married life at Stansted

'*The Meet*', *by W. Pink, 1876.*

coincided with the end of the Victorian era. He was a keen cricketer, and there were frequent matches on the ground in front of the house and even a county match from time to time. He was a remarkable all-round sportsman. As well as being a first-class yachtsman and an excellent shot he was, in the words of his daughter Eleanor Hankey (who was only twenty when he died) capable of riding or driving anything – even two hunters in tandem. When Eleanor met him at the station one evening driving two ponies in similar fashion he was glad to describe her as a chip off the old block. Mary Wilder, although nervous of these exploits and not herself so good on a horse nevertheless, in the words of her daughter, 'loved everything'. She was a keen gardener and had an affection for all animals.

Theirs was in many ways an idyllic existence. They went abroad every year to the south of France or Italy, usually sending on their sailing yacht ahead of them to Nice. They often stayed at Goodwood and at Gordon Castle. They thought nothing of riding some eight miles over the downs to Goodwood for lunch. Two months in Scotland would perfect a year which would end with the duck and pheasants at Stansted.

From 1887 to 1889 the Wilders rented Stansted to Admiral the Earl Clanwilliam, the father of Admiral Sir Herbert Meade-Fetherstonhaugh, the former owner of Uppark. It was at Stansted that Lord Clanwilliam, who later became Commander-in-Chief at Portsmouth, met Miss Fetherstonhaugh. Sir Herbert's brother later became Lord Clanwilliam, and it was thus that Uppark came into the family. It was from Stansted in 1888 that Sir Herbert joined the royal yacht *Britannia* as a naval cadet.

87

20 *The Fire*

IT WAS DURING the ownership of George Wilder's son, George, that the house at Stansted was destroyed by fire said to have been caused either by faulty electric wiring or the leaving of a blowlamp by a plumber in the north-west bedroom. The fire took place on the last day of Goodwood Races in the year 1900. The *Portsmouth Evening News* said it was many a year since such a blaze had been witnessed in the neighbourhood. It lit up the country for miles around. Nearly all the treasures in the house were burnt including the Grinling Gibbons carvings, the Italian frescoes on the ceilings and the pictures of the Queens, Elizabeth and Mary, in the room in which they were supposed to have slept in the Lumley's time.

All the records went too; the books in the library and the many papers which were kept in the large ottoman trunk in the hall. The organ in the hall was of course also destroyed. The only valuable works of art saved were the tapestries of Marlborough's campaigns which Queen Anne had given to Lord Scarbrough in the early eighteenth century. In 1900 these were said to be valued at £30,000. In those days it took some time for fire brigades to arrive and when they did they were seldom able to bring the fire under control. It was fanned by the wind and lasted from eight in the evening until six the next morning. Throughout this time George Wilder superintended operations and helped to fight the flames while Mrs Wilder sat in her landau outside.

The house was rebuilt in 1902 by Arthur Conran Blomfield Jnr in somewhat similar proportions to the original house. Blomfield's work is preferred by many to the double-colonnaded envelope in which Wyatt encased the house in Barwell's time.

During the 1890s the English Renaissance came to be increasingly appreciated in particular for its masculine qualities of vigour and restraint. The key figure in this movement was Sir Reginald Blomfield, Arthur Conran's cousin. Arthur Conran's father, Sir Arthur, was a prolific church architect.

Like a growing number of late nineteenth-century architects, A. C. Blomfield went to university (Cambridge) before entering his father's firm. He also travelled extensively on the Continent. He was principally a city architect, with a large practice of bank buildings. But it was probably his position as Edward VII's architect at Sandringham that attracted the Wilders.

ABOVE *The Blue Drawing Room, restored in 1924.*

RIGHT *Watercolour by Mary, Countess of Bessborough.*

After the fire in 1900.

A. C. Blomfield was not such a scholar as Sir Reginald – he thought that Stansted was erected during the first half of the eighteenth century, for instance – but his design is a handsome essay in the Office of Works idiom, constructed of Rowlands Castle brick and Portland stone dressings. There is a touch of richness in the coupled corner columns of the portico, but otherwise it is remarkably restrained – the west and east elevations being identical.

Although the proportions were almost the same as the seventeenth-century house, except that the new building is six rather than seven bays deep, Blomfield unaccountably chose not to follow Kip's view – the obvious source. Instead, he seems to have based his design on houses like Uffington and Melton Constable illustrated in Belcher and Macartney's *Later Renaissance Architecture in England* (1899–1901) to which Sir Arthur Blomfield and Sons subscribed. Talman, in fact, was not greatly praised by Reginald Blomfield, largely because he obstructed Blomfield's hero, Wren, at Hampton Court.

All the 'very fine oak panelling and carving and plasterwork in high

OPPOSITE *The Library.*

91

relief' in the old house was consumed by fire, 'but sufficient could be seen in comparatively recent photographs to reproduce the former with considerable success,' wrote *The Building News*. 'The plasterwork, though much damaged and disintegrated by heat, was left sufficiently intact to take a complete set of casts before the walls . . . were demolished.' The results can be seen in the library and over the stair.

The four-square plan, with the drawing room (now the music room) immediately behind the entrance hall (then double-storeyed), and the staircase on the north side, was in period. So was the stair – although here Blomfield introduced a Palladian window, perhaps suggested by ones added by Wyatt and Bonomi: authenticity was sacrificed for architectural effect.

During the rebuilding George Wilder stayed at Aldsworth House nearby. Evidently Mr and Mrs George Wilder were popular in the locality. According to the *Hampshire Post & Telegraph* in 1905, they 'had a most enthusiastic welcome home on Saturday on returning from the foreign tour. They arrived from London at Rowlands Castle at 6.24 pm and, driving to the Forest Side Lodge, were met by large crowds. Many carried torches and Havant Town Band played lively airs. The route was lined with fairy lamps while a device on the colonnade bore the words in electric light, "Welcome home".'

Two other printed accounts refer to these years. The social critic and professional snob, T. H.S. Escott, knew the house and described it in some detail in his *Society and the Country House* of 1907. He tells some amusing anecdotes from the century before: 'Among the *habitués* of the place stands

Before the fire.

forth the diplomatist, the stately and polished Sir John Stepney. .... The chief social interest of Stansted lay in its being a place of picturesquely strange and unexpected meetings, set in the beech-wooded park. ...' Escott goes on to tell how Lord North encountered Charles Turner, a Yorkshire MP and implacable opponent whom Rockingham had just made a baronet, in the park:

North: 'You have often accused me of falsehood, but never was I guilty of any lie so gross as that which I have just read in the *Gazette*: "The King has been *pleased* to appoint Lord Rockingham, Mr Fox., Etc. ."' It was only a week or so earlier that Turner had raised roars of laughter in the House against North, whose supporters had called the Opposition 'a rope of sand'. 'The noble lord in the blue ribbon and his companions,' came the retort, 'are a rope of onions, for they stink in the nation's nostrils.'

Unfortunately Escott does not give a source for this exchange at Stansted. Equally his claim that Stansted was a home from home for French Orleanist refugees is intriguing but unsubstantiated. 'Here', he writes, 'the Duc de Broglie and Guizot first made their *début* in an English drawing-room – de Broglie the picture of a French nobleman, Guizot of the intellectual face, but with something of the school usher in his presence.' Could this have been in the time of Barwell or Lewis Way? It seems unlikely, and Escott's observation that the rooms in which the émigrées were

Arthur Blomfield's drawing of the house in 1902.

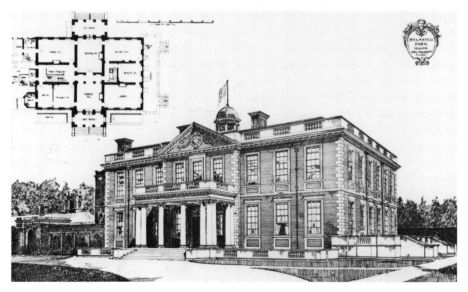

93

The Entrance Hall in 1905.

received had not been altered does not inspire confidence in his accuracy. The unfortunate Wilders are dismissed in a line.

They receive kinder treatment from *The Car Illustrated*, an Edwardian periodical edited by the present Lord Montagu's father. Although, as the title suggests, devoted principally to the automobile, the magazine ran a regular series on country houses, concentrating on the motoring tastes of the owner, his cars and his equipment. Cars were making an important difference to country-house life. On the whole country-house owners could afford them before other people, and the conservative, slow-moving pace of the country house was affected. Cars could travel so much further than horses, with the result that house parties were no longer confined to the estate and each other's company. Individual members could go and dine fifty miles distant if they so wished. The car was of course perfect for the newly-fashionable weekend.

The Car Illustrated correspondent visited Stansted in 1905 and was considerably more deferential than Escott. 'Glancing round the house and its possessions now', he wrote, 'one would hardly credit it as possible that so much had been accomplished, and accomplished so well, in the short

94

space of five years.' Looking at the illustrations from this article we may or may not agree. The centrepiece in the hall was an astonishing, free-standing device that combined a serpent, a globe and an eagle. The hall at that stage went up through two storeys – a typical Edwardian living hall. Ornaments of one kind or another covered every available surface and the fireplaces, all except one subsequently retained by Goodhart-Rendel, were hideous. Mr and Mrs Wilder were shown 'on' (rather than 'in') their 24 HP Mors Car. At the wheel, he wore a Norfolk jacket, check cap and smoked a cigar; she looked feminine in a large picture hat. A particularly unpleasant-looking pug sat on the running board.

The writer was impressed by Stansted's modernity:

Though the house has been faithfully copied from the old building as regards appearance [this is not true, but it is what the Wilders had said] modern and most up-to-date conveniences and methods are found on every hand. The power-house and electric light installation is very complete, and forms one of the most perfect private plants in England lighting as it does some 3,000 to 4,000 large lamps. Mrs Wilder, the energetic chatelaine of Stansted Park, whilst personally supervising and collecting the many treasures, has in no way neglected to provide for the comfort of her guests. All the visitors' rooms are in suite, each containing its own bathroom, and fitted with an outer door on which is fixed a knocker and nameplate for the card of the occupant.

As regards cars, we are given full details: 'Mr Wilder is a thorough automobilist, not only driving his own cars, but capable of doing all repairs. He has trained his electricians to act as motor-men, but always drives and superintends his cars personally.' When the article was written, the Wilders had recently returned from a six-week tour by motor in Scotland. 'Mrs Wilder', the correspondent continues, 'also drives both in town and

Mr and Mrs George Wilder and pug on their 24 HP Mors, 1905.

The Wilders' garage *in 1905.*

country, and for town use has a splendid electric brougham, sumptuously upholstered in rich green plush. The *garage* [in italics as still a French word] at Stansted Park, as befits such an enthusiastic motorist, is complete in every way, and the stud of cars has, indeed, a well-finished resting place.' The garage was in fact in the stables, and the accompanying illustration showed four cars in the courtyard, with a fifth under cover. These were the days in which spare parts were not readily available and had to be made on the garage lathe when required.

In 1912 Wilder sold Stansted to Major Cecil Whitaker. Major Whitaker was also a keen sportsman: not only a fine shot but an ardent fisherman. He kept the stream by the Mill house at Westbourne (which my father put up for sale before he died) well stocked with fish and the woods and the fields with pheasant and partridge. He rented the house for a few years to Captain Quentin Dick and subsequently to his widow who married Lord Howe. As a famous trainer of Labrador retrievers, Lady Howe found at Stansted an ideal place for her work as well as a head keeper in Woolfries who had come to Stansted in Major Whitaker's time and who was of great assistance to her in training her Labradors. It was Major and Mrs Whitaker who made the small Dutch garden between the Chapel and the kitchen garden; and it was they who planted the first Muscat vines in the greenhouses. Major Whitaker also founded with some friends the Emsworth Sailing Club which is still flourishing.

21 *The Bessboroughs*

I MAKE NO attempt in this book to give a full history of the Ponsonby family although, as will be seen later, I do refer to some of its members. But a fairly comprehensive history has already been written by Major-General Sir John Ponsonby and a sequel by his cousin, Sir Charles, and other volumes such as my father's *Lady Bessborough and Her Family Circle, Georgiana* and Arthur Ponsonby's book on *Henry Ponsonby* refer to other distinguished members of the family. They have covered their ground fittingly. The only references I have made to my forebears concern those who were active at Bessborough in Ireland, or may have had some connection with an owner of Stansted or can be seen in the pictures there.

After the burning of Bessborough House in Kilkenny in 1920, which had been in the hands of the family for some 200 years, my parents looked for a place in England to house the family pictures and furniture which had been saved. They visited some sixty-five different houses before they purchased Stansted in 1924. My father's interests in England made it impossible for him to continue to live in Ireland. As Lord Duncannon he had become Conservative MP for Cheltenham in 1911 and a year later for Dover. He played a leading part in the Tariff Reform campaign under Sir Joseph Chamberlain. In 1912 he married my mother, Roberte de Neuflize, daughter of the French banker of that name. During the 1914 war he served at Gallipoli and later on the personal staff of Sir Henry Wilson, the Chief of the Imperial General Staff. In 1917 he was a member of the Milner Mission to Russia.

After the war he accepted a number of directorships in the City which included the Chairmanship of the Margarine Union, the precursor of Unilever, and many other commercial, industrial and financial undertakings. In 1931 at the suggestion of R.B. Bennett, the Conservative Prime Minister in Canada, he was invited by King George V to become Governor-General of the Dominion. One of the many things for which he will be remembered in Canada was his interest in the theatre and while there he founded the Dominion Drama Festival. Until then there had been very little theatre, either professional or amateur, in Canada. My father had always been deeply interested in the stage from the earliest days of private theatricals at Bessborough. He had been a friend of Granville-Barker who was then managing remarkable seasons at the Royal Court

Theatre in Sloane Square. While in Canada my father helped to produce *Hamlet* and *Romeo and Juliet* with the Ottawa Little Theatre and the Montreal Repertory as well as other plays in which I was invited to play the lead. An account of the various productions in the theatre at Stansted is given in Appendix II.

ABOVE *Vere, 9th Earl of Bessborough as Governor-General of Canada in 1935, by Alphonse Jonghers.*
RIGHT *His friend, James de Rothschild – a frequent visitor to Stansted – by George Belcher.*

22 *Rinaldo*

ON PURCHASING STANSTED my father restored and redecorated the house and the Chapel to the plans of my father's old Cambridge friend H.S. Goodhart-Rendel, nephew of Lord Rendel, who became President of the Architectural Association in the year Stansted was bought. Together they used to visit buildings and places of architectural interest in Goodhart-Rendel's chauffeur-driven Rolls-Royce. Called Harry by many, he was known to his more intimate friends, including my parents, as Rinaldo.

As Sir John Summerson says in his entry in the *Dictionary of National Biography*, Goodhart-Rendel became one of the most prominent and interesting figures in his profession due to his personality, scholarship, eloquence and wit as well as his willingness to devote himself assiduously and sympathetically to professional affairs. A scholar, musician, guardsman and architect, he was indeed, as Summerson says, 'distinguished by a patrician elegance, an ironic and slightly plaintive manner of speech, and by the sparkle of a wit issuing from a combination of logical thought and a profound love of paradox'.

'Rinaldo', the architect H. S. Goodhart-Rendel who restored Stansted in 1924–25, by Augustus John.

99

Although with the exception of the Hay's Wharf building, Southwark, Goodhart-Rendel is perhaps still best remembered for his pithy historical writings (especially those which showed an early appreciation of Victorian churches), he had no high opinion of the more conservative Edwardian architects. Reginald Blomfield, by whom he mistakenly took Stansted to be (as already stated it was designed by his cousin, Arthur Conran Blomfield), was dismissed as 'an inferior architect' in *English Architecture Since the Regency* (1953). Consequently over a number of agreeable weekends the Edwardian house was transformed.

Outside, the alterations were subtle: Goodhart-Rendel replaced the glazing bars with the present, thinner ones and opened up the œil de bœufs in the east and west pediments. But inside, the work signalled a distinct change of tone. The dark oak panelling was stripped and 'pickled'; most of the florid fireplaces were replaced (leaving only one – a white-marble confection of swans and cherubs in a south-west bedroom, perhaps out of a sense of historical duty); and the elaborately carved tops to the newel posts of the staircase were taken down.

There is a French note in the Blue Drawing Room, recently redecorated with furniture and pastoral panels (painted by Dirk Dalens) from my mother's flat in Onslow Square. The fireplace, designed by Goodhart-Rendel, was inspired by engravings by Daniel Marot. Although Goodhart-Rendel, with his quick mind, was the least predictable of architects, he was well known as a Francophile. However, at Stansted the French influence was particularly appropriate, since my mother, daughter of the Baron de Neuflize, was herself French.

Two other architectural works belong to this time. Goodhart-Rendel restored the Chapel, elaborately gilding the chancel and giving it a blue, star-studded ceiling based on the Sainte-Chapelle in Paris. His idea was to 'bring out its exotic flavour', according to a note recently discovered by Alan Powers among the architect's papers. He restored the Chapel again in 1947, seven years after a German aircraft carrying a landmine had crashed by the cricket pitch during the Battle of Britain, blowing out the north windows of the chapel and the west windows of the house.

Another war casualty was the theatre for the Society of Stansted Players, modelled on the Duchess Theatre in London and built in 1927 again to Goodhart-Rendel's design. Unfortunately, it did not include any ventilation at the outset. There, as at Cambridge and in Canada, I played many leading roles including Hamlet and Romeo with the Montreal Repertory. The theatre was burnt down after a party for the Home Guard.

It is a reflection of the country-house market in the early 1920s that

Lady Bessborough's repanelled Boudoir.

my father could consider so many possible seats before, after consulting me at the age of ten, choosing Stansted. The house itself, built of red brick and in the style of Queen Anne, does not recall Bessborough, a grey stone mansion. But the wooded landscape was not unlike that in Co. Kilkenny; and at Stansted the Ponsonby family history is told in the pictures and Irish furniture.

23 *Rise of the Ponsonbys*

IN THE ENTRANCE hall, a shrewd, efficient-looking man in Puritanical dress represents the founder of the family fortunes, Sir John Ponsonby. The eldest son of Henry Ponsonby of Haile, in Cumberland, he became Colonel of Horse under Cromwell, and went with the Protector to Ireland – this despite the family motto *Pro rege, lege, grege* (which during the Civil War was mistranslated as *For the king read the people*). Under the Act of Settlement, he was awarded Kildalton, Edmund Dalton's estate, confiscated for his part in the rebellion of 1641. Although Cromwell's period in Ireland is scarcely remarkable for sentiment, Sir John touchingly renamed his property Bessborough, in honour of his second wife, Elizabeth, daughter of Lord Folliott of Ballyshannon.

The second son of his marriage, William, who inherited the Irish estates, was rather belatedly created Baron Bessborough in 1721 for defending Londonderry in the Whig cause against James II. His son, Brabazon, having married Elizabeth, widow of Lord Moore of Tullamore, 'of £2,000 a year estate and £10,000 in ready money', was created a British peer as Baron Ponsonby by George II.

Brabazon Ponsonby was advanced to the Irish earldom of Bessborough in 1739. We know that even before that date he had contemplated rebuilding the house at Bessborough, because Sir Edward Lovett Pearce wrote a memorial about its setting at some stage before his death in 1733. However, the house was not begun until 1744, and work there lasted until 1755, according to Thomas Creevey in a letter of 1828. The architect was a relation by marriage of Sir Edward Lovett Pearce – the gentleman amateur Francis Bindon who painted Dean Swift.

'The mansion of Bessborough', wrote J. M. Brewer in *The Beauties of Ireland* (1825), 'is a spacious structure of square proportions, composed of hewn stone, but the efforts of the architect were directed to amplitude, and the convenience of internal arrangement, rather than to beauty of exterior aspect. ... Viewed as an architectural object, its prevailing characteristic is that of massy respectability.' Creevey, only three years later, responded more enthusiastically: 'This is a charming place', he wrote to Miss Ord, 'I ought to say *as to its position and surrounding scenery –* magnificent.'

After the fire, the house was rebuilt in 1926–30. 'This house in which

Bessborough in Ireland.

I spent so many happy days as a young man was destroyed by the rebels,' wrote Goodhart-Rendel in a note. 'Lord Bessborough in rebuilding it relied on my memory for the character of what new internal detail we were able to put in.' But the family never returned, and Bessborough was purchased by a religious order.

Of all the eighteenth- and nineteenth-century Ponsonbys, William, the second Earl and builder of Bessborough, is the one most fully and most engagingly present at Stansted. As a politician, he followed in the wake of his brother-in-law, the Duke of Devonshire, resigning as Postmaster-General when the latter was dismissed as Lord Chancellor. But at Stansted we see him as a connoisseur, a traveller and a member of the Society of Dilettanti, who was addicted to objects of 'Virtu', according to the *Morning Herald* of 6 August 1782. 'Lord Bessborough is here, who can never grow better or worse, or other than he is,' wrote the Hon. Mrs Hervey in 1777; 'it is incredible what nonsense he talks.'

24 *Liotard's Friend*

BORN IN 1704, Lord Bessborough – the Hon. William Ponsonby as he then was – left on his Grand Tour at the comparatively late age of thirty-two. When he was in Rome, he found himself discussing the merits of a miniature of the Medici Venus with some other Englishmen. The whole party declared it to be the most beautiful object they had seen. As it happened, the artist of the work overheard this eulogy, approached and revealed himself to be Jean-Etienne Liotard, a Swiss who had studied in Paris. The incident is described in François Fosca's life of Liotard, published in 1928. Bessborough – known to Liotard as 'le chevalier Ponsonby' – became his patron, and they went to Constantinople together, where Liotard stayed for five years.

At Constantinople Liotard painted the portrait of Lord Bessborough in Oriental dress which now hangs in the dining room. This shows him as a handsome man, dark in complexion, a turban, red tunic and dark-green coat trimmed with fur. In his belt is a purse, painted with the exquisite detail for which Liotard was celebrated. A companion on the north wall of the room shows Lady Bessborough in Florentine dress. It was not painted until some years later, either in the 1740s or even after Liotard came to England in 1753, since, fifteen years younger than her husband, she did not marry Bessborough until after his return from the East.

'Liotard, the painter, is arrived,' wrote Horace Walpole; '. . . from having lived at Constantinople, he wears a Turkish habit, and a beard down to his girdle: this, and his extravagant prices, which he raised even beyond what he asked in Paris, will probably get him as much money as he covets, for he is avaricious beyond imagination.'

As well as the portrait of his wife, Lord Duncannon employed the artist to make pastels of the other members of his young family, three of which hang in the boudoir. He continued to take an interest in Liotard's work, and bought *La Chocolatière* which had been exhibited at the Academie de Saint-Luc in 1752 and at Christie's in 1774.

The sale of Lord Bessborough's pictures that took place at Christie's on 5–7 February 1801 included other Liotards as well as works by Claude, Poussin, Raphael, Salvator Rosa and van Eyck. The collection was particularly strong in Dutch pictures in which Liotard is known to have dealt.

Having inherited in 1758, the second Earl employed Chambers to build a villa at Roehampton, outside London, in 1760. Sadly, his wife died at the age of thirty-one the same year. Later, however, despite his appearance in the *Town and Country Magazine* of 1776 as the 'kind keeper' of one Mlle Gilbert, a mistress who was reputed to be no less than Princess Amelia, daughter of George II. The portrait by Copley is said originally to have shown the princess on the left, gazing admiringly at the Earl. Presumably this was thought to be *lèse-majesté* because she was painted out and replaced by a screen and urn.

In 1733 Lord Bessborough, following as ever the Duke of Devonshire, protested vehemently against the proposed Irish absentee tax. The first time the third Earl visited Bessborough seems to have been on inheriting in 1793. 'I came here yesterday,' he wrote to his wife on 21 July that year, 'and am indeed very much pleased with the place. . . . The mountains are beautiful over fine wood, & the verdure is the finest that can be seen. I hope I shall be able to make a sketch for you before I go; I mean to confine myself to the 3 days.'

He was equally charmed by the house, its contents and the tenants' reception: 'The house is large & very comfortable, but as you may suppose very old fashioned. There are about 10 or 11 good bedchambers. You would make it very chearful with cutting down the windows & I believe I should agree. There are several good pictures about the house. I have just discovered a Claude Lorraine.'

Princes Amelia, daughter of George II, by Liotard, and William, 2nd Earl of Bessborough, by Copley.

25 Henrietta Frances

THE THIRD EARL, described as 'a man of the most amiable and mild manners' in *Sketches of Irish Political Character* (1779), inherited his father's eye, his principal recreations – apart from playing cards – being sketching and buying prints. 'I am ruined in the number of prints that have been published since I have been absent,' he declared on returning from one of his frequent trips to the Continent in 1792. His wife, Henrietta Frances, whose vivid letters to her retiring mother, Lady Spencer, and her sister, Georgiana, Duchess of Devonshire, are the subject of *Lady Bessborough and Her Family Circle*.

Those to her lover, the young Lord Granville Leveson Gower (they met when she was thirty-three and he eighteen), were published in *Lord Granville Leveson Gower, Private Correspondence*, edited by Castalia, Countess Granville (1916), and include a rapturous description of Bessborough, which she visited for the first time in 1808: '. . . I like this place extremely;

OPPOSITE *Henrietta Frances, Countess of Bessborough, wife of the 3rd Earl, with her sons, Viscount Duncannon and Sir Frederick Ponsonby, by John Hoppner, 1787.*
BELOW *Watercolour of Chatsworth in 1786 by Frederick, Lord Duncannon, later 3rd Earl of Bessborough.*

with a very little expense it might be made *magnificent*, and it is beautiful – et qui pis est, I feel I could do a great deal of good here.'

Lady Bessborough lived until 1821, but her intentions of helping the peasantry were not fulfilled. However, Bessborough proved a useful bolt-hole to take her daughter, Lady Caroline Lamb, after the latter's short-lived and tempestuous adultery with Byron in 1812.

The Victorian Ponsonbys were, typically, more conscientious in visiting their Irish estates than their Georgian and Regency forebears. John William, the fourth Earl, an active supporter of the 1831 Reform Bill and later Melbourne's Home Secretary, was exemplary, according to Creevey, who visited him – then Lord Duncannon – and his family in 1828. 'Lady Duncannon is a charming person, her life here is devoted to looking after everybody, and in making them *clean*, and comfortable and their persons, cloaths, cottages, and everything, and her success is great indeed. *He too*

OPPOSITE *William, 2nd Earl of Bessborough, by Liotard, c. 1742–43.* RIGHT *Henrietta Frances by Sir Joshua Reynolds.*

'*I was the last rose of summer*' – *imaginary self-portrait
by Lady Caroline Lamb.*

in addition to his greater qualities is all after their cleanliness.'

He calculated that, the builder of Bessborough having lived there for two years before his death in 1757, the family had spent just five weeks and two days at the house in the sixty eight years down to 1825. 'My affection for Dear Bessborough remains to the last,' he wrote on 22 September. 'I think I never had a *greater benefit* than in this house.'

The year before his death, in 1847, Bessborough was appointed Lord Lieutenant of Ireland, the first resident Irish landlord to have held office for a generation. But he seems to have built little at Bessborough: his importance to architecture lay in his being First Commissioner of Works when the British Houses of Parliament were being rebuilt.

On the fourth Earl's death, the title passed through three of his sons – John, Frederick and Walter – who became respectively the fifth, sixth and seventh Earls.

Blanche, wife of the eighth Earl, was the youngest daughter of Lady Charlotte Schreiber, the great connoisseur of porcelain and mistress of Canford Manor. My father, Lady Charlotte's grandson, edited extracts from her journals, published in 1952; and some objects from her collection, the greater part of which was bequeathed to the Victoria and Albert Museum, are now at Stansted.

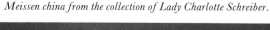

Meissen china from the collection of Lady Charlotte Schreiber.

26 Restoring Stansted

WHILE THE RESTORATION and redecoration of Stansted was taking place in 1924, the family stayed at Deerleap, the house in Rowlands Castle which belonged to Mrs Wilder's brother, Admiral O'Callaghan. As I have said, my father brought to Stansted from Ireland some of the best of the family pictures and some Irish Chippendale furniture and silver which had been saved from the fire at Bessborough. A list of the more interesting pictures in the house is given in Appendix III. The only structural alteration which he made to the house was to erect a first floor in the hall which previously rose to two storeys and then to add the modern bedroom which faces west.

My parents did a great deal of work in the garden. With Tomalin as their head gardener (he had come over from Bessborough in Ireland) they planted a number of cedars and pines (of various sorts) as well as the tulip trees in the arboretum. They reorganized the kitchen gardens, made a shrubbery around a tennis court to the north of the house and extended the lawns on the west and south fronts.

It was at Stansted that my father transcribed all the letters of Henrietta Frances, Lady Bessborough, many of which were published in 1940 in the volume *Lady Bessborough and her Family Circle* which he edited. On arriving for brief spells of leave at Stansted during the early part of the war I remember watching my father taking immense pains to decipher Harriet's writing which seemed quite illegible to all except him. Then after the War I remember him hard at work on the *Diaries of Lady Charlotte Guest* (later Lady Charlotte Schreiber) about whom Sir John Murray published two volumes for him. His last work before he died was to edit the letters of Harriet's sister, Georgiana, Duchess of Devonshire, for which many cases of letters arrived at Stansted from Chatsworth.

Throughout the period of the War my father was concerned with the French Welfare Department of the Foreign Office. In this capacity he frequently saw General de Gaulle and the other Free French leaders, who came down to Stansted to visit the Fighting French naval camp at Emsworth. At the same time he and my mother continued to be active in West Sussex – my father as Chairman of the Chichester Diocesan Fund and my mother as County President of the St John's Ambulance Brigade, Chairman of the Royal West Sussex Hospital (in which my sister Moyra also worked for two years) and as a member of the Bench and various

The Entrance Hall showing the new ceiling and portraits of Lady Maria Fane, wife of the 4th Earl, by Sir Thomas Lawrence and Princess Amelia by Charles Philips, and one of the Marlborough tapestries. The Irish Georgian furniture came from Bessborough in Ireland.

County Council committees. My mother's hard and conscientious work in West Sussex is certainly not forgotten today.

After the War my mother continued her work there while I was serving in the British Embassy in Paris. At the request of Sir Anthony Eden my father became Chairman of the Franco-British Society and continued his work as Chairman of the Council of Foreign Bondholders and the League Loans Committee and as Director of various concerns in the City, some of which he had joined or rejoined after his return from Canada in 1935. He also became Chairman of the Rio Tinto Company and as such he and my mother made visits to Spain and also, in the last year of his life, a return visit to Canada. But like their predecessors at Stansted, my parents were always glad to return home to Sussex and the Forest of Bere.

27 *The Stansted Theatre*

My father's interest in the theatre caused him in 1927 to build a theatre behind the stables at the north end of the house and to form a Society of Stansted Players which included leading members of the Canterbury Old Stagers and the Windsor Strollers as well as some well known professionals and local enthusiasts. Frederick, sixth Earl of Bessborough, had been a founder of the Old Stagers in 1842. Indeed the family had always been interested in theatricals which were often linked with a cricket week. The theatre at Stansted was modelled on the Duchess Theatre (one of the smallest theatres in the West End of London) and up-to-date lighting was installed by Strand Electric. The Players gave performances twice or three times a year: a Shakespeare play in September, some kind of light-hearted entertainment at Christmas and a modern play in the New Year. As will be seen from the list of the plays given in Appendix II, the Players' first production, *She Stoops to Conquer*, was given in the Corn Exchange Theatre, Chichester, since the Stansted Theatre was not ready. But thereafter all performances were given at Stansted, with music provided by the Stansted Players Orchestra under the direction of Mr and Mrs Percy Lewis.

In the autumn of 1929 the Players undertook the heaviest production they ever attempted when they had three performances of *Henry IV (Part I)*. S. R. Littlewood of the *Morning Post* wrote of this production:

Not only in romance of association, but in the beauty and fineness of spirit which pervaded it, yesterday's production of Shakespeare's *Henry IV (Part I)* at the Earl of Bessborough's private theatre at Stansted Park will find a place of its very own in the memories of all who were fortunate enough to see it.

Certainly it would have delighted the heart of Shakespeare himself. He would have rejoiced in the lovely, typically English setting of Lord Bessborough's Sussex home, in the little theatre where, thanks to Mrs Gordon Ives' mural paintings, one passes straight into a world of Fantasy, and in the well-studied feudal pageantry which Lord Bessborough, helped by Mr Rupert Harvey as producer, had managed to get upon his tiny stage with the Ponsonby Arms above the proscenium. Above all, he would have approved the youth and nettle of the chief protagonists, Viscount Duncannon as Prince Hall and his cousin, Mr Arthur Ponsonby, as Hotspur, both of them just sixteen – the same age, it may be remembered, as that of the future Henry V when he returned from suppressing the Welsh rebel-

Lord Bessborough (then Viscount Duncannon) as Romeo (LEFT)
and Hamlet (RIGHT).

lion. The fact that Lord Bessborough himself played Henry IV with quiet dignity, lent a further personal touch to this remarkable performance. . . .

In *The Younger Generation*, which was put on in January 1931, I played the part of Reggie Kennion, the young man who constantly during the play expresses his desire to to go Canada. This wish was unexpectedly fulfilled when two months later I went there with my parents on my father's appointment as Governor-General. During my father's term of office in Canada the Theatre was closed except for one production of *Twelfth Night* in 1932.

When the time came to choose a play for the autumn production of 1939, the international clouds looked so black that the Stansted Players hesitated before making any plans. It was felt, however, that to abandon ordinary peace-time avocations before the War was certain was only to encourage pessimism about the future. It was accordingly decided to proceed tentatively, and *The Rose without a Thorn* by Clifford Bax was chosen for production. Robert Speaight promised to produce, and the Players duly arrived at Stansted on 21 August to start rehearsals. These continued normally until Thursday evening the 24th, when Miss Ann Casson was already giving a notable performance as Katherine Howard. On the 25th, however, the situation was so grave that it was decided to abandon the production. The Theatre, the Green Room and adjoining dressing-rooms were all destined in case of war to be occupied by the children from Services' House, Portsmouth, and their arrival was to be expected at any moment. That it was hopeless to attempt to go ahead was made clear on Sunday, the 27th, when several members of the cast were called up for active service.

Since the Theatre had been built in 1927, plays had been produced regularly twice or three times a year except when my parents were in Canada. Among those who took part in the plays besides Robert Speaight, Ann Casson, members of the family and well known amateurs, were Margaretta Scott, Basil Bartlett, E. Martin Browne and his wife Henzie Raeburn, as well as Dulcie Grey who accepted to marry Michael Denison when playing in *School for Scandal* at Stansted.

After the outbreak of war the Theatre was used in the daytime by the evacuee children from Portsmouth who occupied the north and stable wings of the house; and after the formation of the Home Guard it was used by them of an evening for various purposes including that of a miniature rifle range.

In 1942 the Theatre was accidentally destroyed by fire attributed to cigarette ends carelessly dropped by members of the Home Guard when attending the showing of a training film in it one evening. All the contents of the theatre were destroyed including the furniture from my father's house in Eaton Square which was stored on the stage. All that remains are the murals in the foyer painted by Mrs Gordon Ives.

My own memories of the plays at Stansted are too numerous to relate here. My earliest recollections are of Ralph Alderson – an amateur actor who was said to be even more effective than Sir Herbert Beerbohm Tree – playing most of Tree's parts. On more than one occasion Ralph was offered tempting professional engagements, as indeed I was myself, but for various reasons neither of us ever took them up. I remember in particular Ralph's playing of Bottom in *A Midsummer Night's Dream*, his sinister Svengali in du Maurier's *Trilby*, his Shylock in *The Merchant of Venice* as well as his Falstaff in *Henry IV (Part I)*. These were among the first plays in which I myself acted taking the parts respectively of Oberon, Little Billee, Lorenzo and Prince Hal. But I also vividly recall the production of Bridie's *Tobias and the Angel* which was produced by Martin Browne and in which Caroline Paget played Sara ('You have the mind of a child

LEFT *Viscount Duncannon as Prince Hal and Arthur Ponsonby
as Hotspur in* Henry IV *Part i.*
RIGHT *Viscount Duncannon as the Archangel Raphael in* Tobias
and the Angel by James Bridie.

and the instincts of an animal') and I the part of the Archangel Raphael
– which I had already taken in productions of the play in Ottawa and
Montreal.

Then who could forget Margaretta Scott as Rosaline in *Love's Labour's
Lost*? Playing Berowne opposite her I found her rendering of the closing
lines extraordinarily beautiful:

> . . . that's the way to choke a jibing spirit,
> Whose influence is begot of that loose grace
> Which shallow laughing hearers give to fools:
> A jest's prosperity lies in the ear
> Of him that hears it, never in the tongue
> Of him that makes it . . .

28 The War and After

ENEMY ACTION AT Stansted during the War was considerable. Some eighty-five bombs, innumerable incendiaries and four aircraft fell on the estate. On one occasion during the Battle of Britain incendiaries ringed the house. On another a German aircraft carrying a landmine fell at the south-west corner of the cricket ground and exploded, killing all the crew and mortally wounding Gilbert Elliot, a friend and helicopter pilot, who was staying at Stansted. My mother and sister watched this happen from the steps of the house. It was on this occasion that the north windows of the Chapel and all the west windows of the house were blown out and all the glass of the greenhouses in the garden broken. The Chapel had to be closed, and services were held in the vaulted crypt which is the only reminder of the older house on the present site. However, after the war, in 1947, the Chapel was again restored by Goodhart-Rendel. In addition to the bomb damage the timberwork had been affected by dry rot during the seven years it had been closed.

While serving on the staff of General McNaughton, the Canadian Commander-in-Chief in 1940–41, I brought him to stay the odd night at Stansted. His own headquarters were at Leatherhead in Surrey. I used to chaff him by saying that he ought to come home for a weekend to see something of the front line! A dummy airfield similar to Portsmouth had been erected at Thorney three miles to the south of Stansted and it was this that attracted so many enemy raiders. The park was often occupied by troops. They came in especially large numbers before the invasion of Normandy in June, 1944, as they may have done before Agincourt over 500 years previously. General Eisenhower's own headquarters before D-Day were in a fort on Portsdown hill barely six miles from Stansted.

Before the last war the Princess Royal and the late Lord Harewood frequently stayed with my parents at Stansted for Goodwood Races; and the Queen, now Queen Elizabeth the Queen Mother, spent a night there in December 1939. They all planted trees as have many other distinguished visitors before and since. Numerous friends have from time to time come to shoot at Stansted including my mother's Neuflize relations from France and my wife's relations from the United States. Sir Anthony Eden came over more than once after the War while he was living at Binderton. I hope it is not indiscreet to record that shooting one Boxing

LEFT *The wedding of Lord and Lady Duncannon in Paris in 1948,*
with Vere, 9th Earl of Bessborough (left) and Charles A. Munn,
the bride's father (between the bride and groom).
RIGHT *Lady Bessborough by A. Vidal Quadras.*

Day while he was Foreign Secretary he told us he was glad that Sir Winston
Churchill had decided not to hold a Cabinet Meeting that day for this
had enabled him to help kill some of the cocks in Stansted Forest. Lord
Thorneycroft too while Minister for Defence would join the guns in the
early sixties when he and Lady Thorneycroft occupied the Clock Tower
flat, and every year since I became his Parliamentary Secretary in 1963,
Lord Hailsham, the Lord Chancellor, has come to shoot cocks over the
New Year.

Other guns have included the King of Greece, Bernard, the late Duke
of Norfolk, and the Duke of Richmond who came over from Arundel and
Goodwood on occasion as their forebears had done before them. The late
Earl of Scarbrough also stayed at Stansted and walked through the Forest
and along the avenues first laid out by his ancestor. The late Earl of
Spencer stayed on more than one occasion and discussed the famous Northampton election in which his forbear opposed Lord Halifax, and vast
sums of money were expended on both sides.

Another visitor was Viscount Lewisham, now Lord Dartmouth, who
came with his wife, Raine, now Countess Spencer, to look at Racton which

had passed to his family two hundred years previously. Others who have had an enduring attachment to the forest and the duck ponds have included the late Lord Portal of Hungerford, the Chief of the Air Staff during the Second World War, who lived only a few miles away at West Ashling. Lord Cowdray too would come over from Cowdray Park, Midhurst, as well as many Commanders-in-Chief, Portsmouth, ever since the Fitzalan Earls of Arundel were Admirals of the West and South in the fourteenth century. The duck ponds have a special attraction, but another fascination have been the woodcock in the forest. They used to be more plentiful than perhaps anywhere in south-east England. Therefore while there is now no hawking, no longer any wild boar but still many roe and fallow deer, Stansted's tradition as a hunting lodge is still very much alive today; and Leslie Buckle, the present head keeper, looks after the birds as skilfully as Silvester tended the King's falcons eight hundred years previously.

LEFT *Lord and Lady Bessborough and Rio the macaw, by John Edwards.*
ABOVE *Lord Bessborough, first British Vice-President of the European Parliament, with George Thomas (later Viscount Tonypandy), Speaker of the House of Commons, 1983.*

29 *The Faerie Queene*

IT WAS IN 1959 that my friend, Ronald Armstrong, drew my attention to a sale at Christie's at which first editions of the two volumes of *The Faerie Queene* were to be sold. The first volume had been carefully annotated in what appeared to be a scholarly Elizabethan hand, and Armstrong suggested that I go and look at it. After all, I could be said to be descended both from the poet and his publisher, William Ponsonby, who dwelt in St Paul's Churchyard 'neere unto the great north dore': and this was the most important work to come off William's presses. As head of the Ponsonby family I had often thought that William must have been one of its most distinguished members. In the end it was through John F. Fleming of New York City that I came into possession of these volumes with the second of which Ponsonby had also bound up the first edition of *Colin Clouts Come Home Againe*.

It was likewise my friend Armstrong who in 1962 told me of the publication of Graham Hough's *A Preface to* The Faerie Queene. As the proud possessor of the only copy of the first volume of Edmund Spenser's poem with apparently contemporary annotations, I was interested to read Mr Hough's book for it seemed to me that these notes confirmed to some extent his own interpretation of the allegorical character of a poem which was undoubtedly the greatest work of 'the Poet's Poet'. At the same time it was a poem which seemed to me to give, perhaps, the most vivid image of Elizabethan England.

I cannot claim that my ancestor, William Ponsonby, discovered Edmund Spenser. This good fortune must go to his friend, Gabriel Harvey, Edward Kirke in Cambridge or perhaps to the Earl of Leicester in London. It was in any case Hugh Singleton who published *The Shepherds Calendar* in 1579. However, Ponsonby did publish all his other works – ten volumes in all – and, having examined the list compiled by the British Museum of all his known publications – which of course also included Sidney's *Arcadia* – I would be fascinated to see written a life of this William and to know how he came to produce these various works, for they cover a very wide field. In addition to Spenser and Sidney, they range from a first English translation of Machiavelli to Taverner's experiments concerning fish and fruit – to say nothing of 'a profitable boke declaring dyvers approved remedies to take out spots and staines'. Altogether Ponsonby printed some sixty known volumes, from which it is clear that not only were his interests wide and deep but his discernment considerable; and once the first volume of *The Faerie Queene* appeared Spenser remained faithful to him as his publisher.

As will already have been gathered, my own family's relationship with the poet goes back to my great-great-great-grandmother, Henrietta Frances, daughter of the first Earl Spencer and wife of the third Earl of Bessborough. In the *Prothalamion* Spenser refers to the 'house of auncient fame' with which he was connected – that is to say the Spencers of Althorp – and it was Gibbon who declared that:

... the nobility of the Spencers has been illustrated and enriched by the trophies of Marlborough; but I exhort them to consider *The Faerie Queene* as the most precious jewel of their coronet.

It is in *Colin Clout* that Edmund hymns the praises of the three daughters of Sir John Spencer whom he describes as his cousins:

Ne less praisworthie are the sisters three,
The honor of the noble familie:
Of which I meanest boast my self to be ...

Spenser speaks of 'their beauties amorous reflexion': *Charillis*:

A fairer Nymph yet never saw mine eie:
She is the pride and primrose of the rest ...

But in admiration of *Amaryllis* the poet tells the shepherd:

... what ever thou hast heard to be
In this or that praysd diversly apart,
In her thou maist them all assembled see,
And seald up in the threasure of her hart.

Moreover to each of Sir John's daughters Spenser dedicated one of his other poems. In 1590, soon after the publication of *The Faerie Queene*, William Ponsonby brought out the *Muiopotmos* or *The Fate of the Butterflie* which Spenser dedicated to Elizabeth, who had become Lady Carey:

... for so excellent favours as I have received at your sweet handes ... Therefore I have determined to give my selfe wholly to you, as quite abandoned from my selfe, and absolutely vowed to your services ...

To Alice, who became Lady Strange, and who acknowledged 'some private bands of affinitie' with the poet, he addressed in 1591 *The Teares of the Muses* – a poem which Shakespeare described in *A Midsummer Night's*

Dream as 'some satire keen and critical'. In the same year another satire on court vices and follies, the *Prosopopoia*: or *Mother Hubberds Tale*, was presented to the third daughter, Ann, as Lady Compton and Mountegle, for:

the humble affection and faithful duetie, which I have alwaies professed, and am bound to beare to that House, from whence yee spring . . .

Another family interest lies in the fact that John Keats, who was, as I have said, inspired to write some of his finest work – *The Eve of St Agnes* and *The Eve of St Mark* – as a result of his visit to Stansted in January 1819, probably wrote his very first lines *In Imitation of Spenser*. Moreover, if Spenser wrote most of *The Faerie Queene* 'in the wild and solitary country of Ireland' – a country with which, as has been seen, my own family, had been familiar over the generations – it is interesting that during the year of the publication of his great romantic epic in 1590 he paid a prolonged visit to the neighbourhood of Alton in Hampshire which is not so far across the county border from our own home in Sussex. According to Aubrey it was 'in this delicate sweete aire where he enjoyed his muse and writt good part of his verses'.

Finally it is a curious fact that this particular volume of *The Faerie Queene*, which is believed to be the finest in existence, was for long in the hands of the Weller-Poley family who lived not only at Boxted in Suffolk, where their library is still housed, but also, before the Second World War, on the Holme Farm at Stansted on the edge of our own enchanted forest, where I have seen, if not broken, the golden bough, divined the temptations of the Bower of Bliss and known the kind of light-obscuring forest which led the Red Cross Knight astray.

The Faerie Queene was indeed Spenser's crowning achievement and Ponsonby's most important publication.

LONDON
Printed for William Ponfonbie.
1 5 9 0.

The colophon of the publisher, William Ponsonby, from Lord Bessborough's first edition of Spenser's The Faerie Queene.

KEY

Lord Hailsham receiving a brace of pheasants from the head
keeper, surrounded by many of those associated with Stansted.
Painting by Nigel Purchase, 1983.

81 Mr B. House, woodsman
82 Mr R. Smith, tenant farmer
83 Mrs M. Smith, wife of tenant farmer
84 The Rev. P. Baden, vicar in charge of
   St Pauls Chapel
85 Mrs P. Baden, wife of vicar
86 Mrs D. Sheridan, tenant
87 Mr C. Sheridan, tenant
88 Kate Sheridan, tenant
89 Mrs S. Dowsett, farm employee
90 Mr D. Dowsett, farm employee
91 Mrs M. Sutton, wife of woodsman
92 Philip Sutton, son of woodsman
93 Mr M. Sutton, woodsman
94 The Count Lanza, tenant and nephew
   of Lord Bessborough
95 The Countess Lanza, tenant and niece
   of Lord Bessborough
96 Miss Sheree Billing, nanny/children's
   nurse
97 Riccardo Lanza, Lord Bessborough's
   niece's son
98 Aleramo Lanza, Lord Bessborough's
   niece's son
99 The Lady Moyra Browne, DBE, sister
   of Lord Bessborough
100 Lady George, tenant
101 Mr Y. Petsopoulos, Lord
    Bessborough's son-in-law

102 The Lady Charlotte Petsopoulos,
    Lord Bessborough's daughter
103 Alexis Petsopoulos, Lord
    Bessborough's grandson
104 Sally George, daughter of Captain
    T. A. George
105 Richard George, son of Captain
    T. A. George
106 Mrs. R. Housden, estate secretary
107 Mrs. L. Mayes, cook–secretary
108 Mr A. McCluskey, retired farm
    employee
109 Mr P. Harding, son of maintenance
    manager
110 Miss L. Harding, daughter of
    maintenance manager
111 Miss C. Hurlin, estate manager
112 Mrs J. Browne, tenant and wife of
    Lord Bessborough's nephew
113 Harry Ponsonby, son of Lord
    Bessborough's cousin
114 Natasha Browne, daughter of Lord
    Bessborough's nephew
115 Frederick Ponsonby, son of Lord
    Bessborough's cousin
116 Chloe Ponsonby, daughter of Lord
    Bessborough's cousin
117 Mrs A. Ponsonby, wife of Lord
    Bessborough's cousin

118 Mrs C. Offord, tenant
119 Mr D. Browne, tenant and Lord
    Bessborough's nephew
120 Harriet Browne, daughter of Lord
    Bessborough's nephew
121 Emily Scott, resident
122 Lucy Scott, resident
123 Peter Clark, son of head sawyer
124 Mr R. Stenhouse, retired head bailiff
125 Mr O. Bailey, retired woodsman
126 Owen Bailey, son of retired woodsman
127 Nicola Dowsett, daughter of farm
    employee
128 Mr D. Harding, maintenance manager
129 Mr N. Purchase, artist of painting
130 Lisa Burt, daughter of farm employee
131 Andrew Dowsett, son of farm employee
132 Mr Hugh Graham, photographer
133 Mr E. McCloy, husband of ex-employee
134 Mrs M. McCloy, ex-employee
A Flag of European Parliament
B Peacock 'Old Joe'
C Macaw 'Rio'
D Miller
E Diver
F Tobias
G Katie
H Bonnet
I Meg

30 *Space Age Theatre*

> . . . theatres and temples lie
> Open unto the fields, and to the sky;
> All bright and glittering in the smokeless air.
>   (William Wordsworth: *Sonnet* XXXVI)

AFTER THE SECOND World War there was some discussion as to whether I should rebuild the Stansted Theatre, but this did not prove practical and no decision was taken. However in the late fifties I was approached by Leslie Evershed-Martin, a Chichester optician and former Mayor of the city with the proposition that a modern theatre with a thrust stage should be built in Oaklands Park outside the city.

In particular I well remember how one Saturday afternoon in February 1960, I happened to be flying with my wife to New York, partly on ATV business and partly to see my father-in-law in Florida, and then on to a blast-off at Cape Canaveral. We arrived at the St Regis Hotel in New York at 7 pm and were due to dine late with my sister-in-law. It was only while over the Atlantic that I remembered that Leslie Evershed-Martin had, at the suggestion of Sir Tyrone Guthrie, written to Sir Laurence Olivier, then acting in Anouilh's *Becket* in New York, inviting him to become the Chichester Festival Theatre's first Artistic Director.

The Theatre was to be built on the lines of the open stage at Stratford, Ontario. It had taken a few months for Leslie to persuade me of the feasibility of the project, despite the fact that I was very well disposed in principle – ever since my father's Theatre had been burnt down and also because of the family's connections with Canada. But in 1959, when Leslie first approached me, theatres were being torn down in London. The St James's had been the most recent example and I was involved in the famous debate in the House of Lords in which Vivien Leigh, then wife of Sir Laurence Olivier, intervened.

Partly as a result of the growth of television, the building of another

---

OPPOSITE *Roberte, Countess of Bessborough, with her children,
Viscount Duncannon, Lady Moyra Ponsonby and the Hon.
Desmond Ponsonby, by Oswald Birley, 1922.*

theatre was, in the eyes of some property owners, a risky concept. Moreover, what had the theatre to do with Television and the Space Age? We already had more professional theatres per head of the population than any other country in the world.

However, I remembered on the 'plane that Leslie had sent to Sir Laurence proposed plans of the theatre drawn up by the architects Powell and Moya; and I thought that, however fraught with difficulties the project might be, there could be no harm in trying to see Larry while I was in New York in order to get his first reactions. I had seen him in Christopher Fry's *Venus Observed* as the Ducal astronomer (surely he knew something of the Space Age?), I had met him at ATV's Wood Green Studios when he was performing in *John Gabriel Borkman* by Ibsen – and I was encouraged by support from Hugh 'Binkie' Beaumont of H.M. Tennent, as well as from Norman Collins and Lew (later Lord) Grade of ATV.

Neville Blond, the Chairman of the English Stage Company, as well as the Arts Council and other friends, said they would support us too. I think they came to agree that, provided we had a first class Artistic Director, a theatre of the size proposed seating 1,360 people and built in the most beautiful part of West Sussex at reasonable cost, thanks to the McAlpines, might well be an economic proposition as well as a cultural success.

So on arrival in New York I rang Larry up at his flat to ask whether he was interested in talking about Chichester and whether I could see him. He replied 'yes' but that he was about to go round to the theatre to make-up. Could I come about 11 pm? I said 'Yes', although I felt somewhat exhausted after the Atlantic flight – not then in a jet but an old piston-engined machine. After all, 11 pm would be 4 am by the time I had taken off from London.

I arrived at the Century Theatre at Curtain fall at 11 pm and went straight to Larry's dressing room where he asked whether I would have supper in his apartment with him and his future wife, Joan Plowright. We could then look at the plans.

After supper the drawings were laid on the floor. Could the pillars of the interior stage be altered? They might obscure the view of some of the audience. We talked for some hours and then I returned to the hotel, not having slept, and telephoned to Leslie in Chichester. It was a Sunday morning. I said that I thought Larry *was* interested, and we discussed some of the detailed points. I felt we were home and dry. And over the past years I think we can say that the record of our Theatre has lived up to our best expectations. It is still one of the most outstanding Festival Theatres in the world.

ABOVE *Chichester Festival
Theatre.* LEFT *Joan Plowright
and Laurence Olivier in* Uncle
Vanya *at the Festival Theatre,
1962.*

What *is* Chichester's place in the world? Stratford can be described as the theatre of Shakespeare; the National the international theatre of Great Britain; the Aldwych had been described as the theatre of cruelty; the Royal Court the theatre for writers; and in Sir John Clements' own words (how admirable a successor to Sir Laurence) Chichester, the theatre for actors.

But Chichester is, of course, an international theatre too; and from 1963 to 1965 housed the National Theatre Company itself. *Uncle Vanya* and *The Cherry Orchard* by Chekov, Shaw's *St Joan* and *Heartbreak House*, Shaffer's *The Royal Hunt of the Sun* and *Black Comedy*, Shakespeare's *Othello*, *Macbeth* and *The Tempest*, Arden's *The Workhouse Donkey*, Anouilh's *The Fighting Cock*, Eliot's *The Cocktail Party*, Wilder's *The Skin of Our Teeth* and Ustinov's *The Unknown Soldier and his Wife*, to mention only some of our productions, are all internationally well-known plays, and at Chichester they were superbly performed by internationally famous stars. They included Olivier, John Clements, Sybil Thorndike, Joan Plowright, Michael Redgrave, Michael Aldridge, Eileen Atkins, Albert Finney, Joan Greenwood, Peter Ustinov and Alec Guinness. And I trust many future stars will also perform there.

It takes some time to get through the whole alphabet, but let me continue by recalling the names of Rosemary Harris, Millicent Martin, Keith Michell, John Neville, Joyce Redman, Prunella Scales, Robert Stephens, Billy Whitelaw, to name only some of the better known. And there was Margaret Leighton as Cleopatra, Maggie Smith as Margery Pinchwife, Alastair Sim in Pinero and Topol in Brecht! What more could anyone ask?

And because of our actors and the size and original structure of the theatre, we had also been able to call on the best directors and designers too – not only Olivier and Clements, Guinness and Ustinov, but Norman Marshall, Lindsay Anderson, Michael Benthall, Peter Coe, William Gaskell, John Dexter, Robert Chetwyn, Peter Dews, William Chappell, Michael Annals, Alan Jagg, Peter Rice and Sean Kenny. And now we have as Artistic Director our much respected Patrick Garland and highly successful executive producer in John Gale.

And what a tremendous emergency job the two Peters (Coe and Rice) did with *An Italian Straw Hat* in 1967! Chichester should be a theatre for unconventional production techniques. It should be a kind of super circus-like theatreama (if I may coin the word) with effective lighting and stereophonic sound. It gives unusual scope for the actors – and a sense of participation too – for the audience.

It is therefore not surprising as I travel the world to find that Chichester has become known as one of the most fascinating theatres on this particular planet. Ontario's Stratford, whose company had itself performed successfully in Chichester, and Minnesota's Minneapolis, assume a kind of parentage. (How much did we owe to Sir Tyrone Guthrie!) But I have found too, that in the Soviet Union, from Moscow to Novosibirsk, from Tibilisi to Irkutsk, and in South East Asia, from Peshawar to Colombo and Singapore, we have become known not only to those concerned with the theatre. In the West, where news travels faster and more freely, we are famous throughout Europe, the United States and in South America – especially thanks to Peter Shaffer's 'Conquistadores'.

Indeed, everywhere I have been in the last twenty years talking about Britain's scientific achievements (I was lured partly away from the Arts and the drama when I became a Minister for Science in 1963), I found that people knew I had something to do with Chichester and asked how the theatre was faring.

But it is not only because of the actors and the plays performed in our space-age theatre that we have gained international renown, but also because of the celebrity concerts in which so many great names have appeared – Yehudi Menuhin to Joyce Grenfell, Oistrach to Emlyn Williams, Rostropovitch to Willi Boskovsky – and the Royal Philharmonic Orchestra – to mention only a few.

Now that we have become so well known we have to keep up our standards. This has not been easy. There are only relatively few internationally known stars in the world and since the establishment of three National Theatre auditoria and three Royal Shakespeare theatres it is not so easy to attract the top stars. But we must continue to keep them interested so that we never lack for top talent – and good supporting talent too. Otherwise we shall die. I believe that only stars can fill a theatre of Chichester's size for an economic number of performances – if we are not to draw heavily on the taxpayer. And that is why in Chichester the actor, perhaps even more than the playwright, *must* come first. That is why we have become 'the theatre for actors' and why I think that by and large, we must remain so, although at the suggestion of Hugh (now Lord) Cudlipp, we are now rightly known as 'the theatre for all seasons'. It has been a great joy over the years to welcome many of those associated with the theatre to the enchanted forest which is Stansted.

31 *The Sun Goes Down*

I will hold my house in the high wood
Within a walk of the sea,
And the men that were boys when I was a boy
Shall sit and drink with me.
(Hilaire Belloc, *The South Country*)

WHEN MY FATHER died at Stansted in March 1956, my wife and I decided, by making economies wherever possible, to do our utmost to keep the house and park in good trim. The Chancellor of the Exchequer and the rulers in the Kremlin being willing, I hope we may continue to do so until we die. Mr Tomalin, the famous head gardener who wrote week by week in the *Gardeners' Chronicle*, died in 1954, but his successor, Mr Crockford, and now Mr Koppert, although with a much reduced staff carry on most

Cricket at Stansted.

The swimming pool surrounded by capitals from the old Wyatt House.

efficiently with the assistance of John Rowe, the head forester, who looks after the woods and the trees. Douglas Harding with Bernard and Pearl House care for the mansion, while Mr Stenhouse, the bailiff, in his time and then Gordon Gaunt did their utmost to make the farm break even year by year. Catherine Hurlin skilfully manages the Estate. My wife and I have made no structural alterations to the house except to convert the old stables into a cricket and tea pavilion for the people on the estate and for those visiting the park and gardens when they are open to the public, and transforming the old laundry and bakery into a Bathing Pavilion with access to the swimming pool surrounded by statues we have collected and the capitals from the old Wyatt House found in the woods nearby. In 1958 we planted an avenue to the east (similar to that which can be seen in Kip's view) in memory of my father.

For the Festival of Sussex in 1951 I made a dramatic arrangement of Hilaire Belloc's *The Four Men*, which was performed throughout the county and subsequently broadcast by the BBC. Robert Speaight produced and played the part of Belloc himself with remarkable insight. Ian Wallace of Glyndebourne and Drury Lane was a rousing success as the sailor, bringing the house down with such famous Belloc songs as 'In Sussex hills where I was bred' to music especially composed be my cousin, David Ponsonby.

The newly-planted avenue in the East Park.

It occurred to me, while preparing this adaptation that Stansted with its long avenue facing west must in truth be 'the place where the sun goes down', and I seemed, in Belloc's words, to know what made it so glorious. The Park lies, indeed, in the westernmost part of the county a few miles south of Harting beyond which, as Belloc said, there are 'only shapeless things'. A few acres of Stansted and the village of Rowlands Castle lie in Hampshire. Within the triangle made up by Rowlands Castle to the west, Forestside to the north and Stansted House to the east there extends some thousand acres of forest made up largely of beech which remind the visitor of the verse from the great poem at the end of *The Four Men* so superbly spoken by Robert Speaight during the Festival of Sussex:

> The beeches know the accustomed head
> Which loved them, and a peopled air
> Beneath their benediction spread
> Comforts the silence everywhere.
>   For native ghosts return and these
>   Perfect the mystery in the trees.

The people of Chichester, Westbourne, Havant and Portsmouth, and many from farther afield, are able to stroll under the beeches and along the public footpaths which cross the park and woods. Of a Saturday or Sunday afternoon they may watch a cricket match in front of the house (the Stansted Cricket Club has a fine record!), admire the view and see the sun go down at the end of the long avenue (said to be the only two-mile beech avenue in England) and look out towards the Isle of Wight, as Earl Godwin may have done 900 years ago, or back towards the house as Charles II did at dawn over 600 years later. Then indeed the 'native ghosts return' recalling the forest courts of the Earls of Arundel and Henry II's new buildings there; the Lumleys who built the first glorious house on the present site; George Halifax and Marianne whom he loved; the Indian Nabob, Barwell, and his riches from the East and the Duke of Clarence and his preference for Resurrection Pie. Then, too, we may remember the silver spoons of Lewis Way; George Wilder and his tandem of two hunters and the poet Keats composing lines for *The Eve of St Mark* in the Chapel beyond the trees – the trees beneath which are buried my parents and my brothers who also knew the magic and the mystery of the woods.

The main avenue.

Appendix I — OWNERS OF STANSTED FROM THE CONQUEST TO THE PRESENT DAY

EARL GODWIN
(father of King Harold)
d. 1053

THE EARLS OF ARUNDEL

(1) HOUSE OF MONTGOMERY
Roger de Montgomery, *1st Earl* = Mabel de Bellême
d. 1094

Robert (de Bellême), *3rd Earl* = Agnes de Ponthieu
attd. 1113, d. 1131

Hugh de Montgomery, *2nd Earl*
d. unm. 1098

(2) HOUSE OF D'AUBIGNY
William d'Aubigny, *1st Earl* = Adeliz, the Queen Dowager
(also styled Earl of Sussex   d. 1151
and Earl of Chichester)
d. 1176

William, *2nd Earl* = Maud, widow of Roger de Clare,
d. 1193   Earl of Hertford

William = Mabel, sister of
3rd Earl Ranulph le Meschin,
d. 1220   Earl of Chester

Hugh, *4th Earl* = Isobel, daughter of
d. 1243   William de Warenne,
         Earl of Surrey

Isabel = John Fitzalan,
      still living 1286

(3) HOUSE OF FITZALAN
John Fitzalan, *1st Earl*
d. 1267

John, *2nd Earl*
d. 1272

Richard, *3rd Earl* = Alasia di Saluzzo
d. 1302

Edmund, *4th Earl* = Alice de Warenne,
attd. and d. 1326 | heiress to Earls of Surrey and Sussex

Richard, restored as *5th Earl* = Eleanor
d. 1376

Richard, *6th Earl*
beheaded 1397

Thomas, restored = Beatrice, nat. dau. of
as *7th Earl*, d. 1415   King John I of Portugal

(John = Eleanor, Baroness Mautravers
d. 1379 | *suo jure*, d. 1405)

(John
d. 1391)

John, Lord Mautravers, = Eleanor, dau. of
8th Earl, d. 1421 | Sir John Berkeley

John, *9th Earl*
d. 1435

Humphrey, *10th Earl*
d. unm. 1438

William, *11th Earl*
uncle and h., d. 1488

Thomas, *12th Earl* = Margaret Woodville
d. 1524

William, *13th Earl* = Anne Percy
d. 1544

Henry, *14th Earl* = Catherine Grey
Last Fitzalan Earl, d. 1579 |

KEY

d.s.p.: *decessit sine prole*
(died without issue)

d.v.p.: *decessit vita patris*
(died in the lifetime
of his father)

suo jure: in one's own right

HOUSE OF LUMLEY

Thomas Howard, = Mary Fitzalan   Jane Fitzalan = John, *6th Lord Lumley* = Elizabeth d'Arcy   (Henry Fitzalan, Lord
Duke of Norfolk   d. 1557)   d. 1576   d.s.p. 1609   d. *c.* 1617   Mautravers, d. 1556)
beh. 1572

John was succeeded by his cousin,
Sir Richard Lumley, great-grandson of 4th Lord Lumley,
created Viscount Lumley = Frances Holland
d. 1661

(John = Mary, dau. and co-h. of
d.v.p. 1658 | Sir Henry Compton)

Richard, 2nd Viscount Lumley = Frances, daughter   (Henry Lumley, General and   **EARLS OF SCARBROUGH**
and *1st Earl* of Scarbrough   and h. of   MP for Arundel)
d. 1721   Sir Henry Jones

Henry, Viscount   Richard,   (Thomas, *3rd Earl* = Frances, dau. of   James Lumley,   (Mary = George Montague
Lumley   *2nd Earl*   (Lumley-Saunderson) |Earl of Orkney)   Col. and MP   d. 1726 Earl of Halifax
unm. 1710   d. umn. 1739   d. 1766   d. 1739)

(Richard, *4th Earl* = Barbara, sister   George Montague-Dunk = Ann, h. of   **EARLS OF HALIFAX**
d. 1782   and h. of   *2nd Earl* of Halifax | Sir Thomas Dunk
Sir George Savile)   d. 1771

Anna, nat. dau. = Richard Archdall
sold Stansted in 1781 to:

Richard Barwell
THE INDIAN NABOB
d. 1804
when Stansted was sold to:

Lewis Way = Mary Drewe
d. 1840 |

Drusilla

Lewis Way sold Stansted in 1826 to:

(George Wilder) = Augustine = Charles Dixon
d. 1871   d. 1855

(George Wilder
d. 1856)

George Wilder = Mary O'Callaghan
d. 1896 | d. 1942

George Wilder = Una Hodgson
sold Stansted in 1912 to:

Major Cecil Whitaker
who sold Stansted in 1924 to:

(Edward, 8th Earl of Bessborough = Blanche Guest)   **EARLS OF BESSBOROUGH**

Vere, *9th Earl* of Bessborough = Roberte de Neuflize   Myles Ponsonby = Rita Longfield
d. 1956   d. 1917

Frederick, = Mary Munn   Desmond   Moyra = Denis Browne   George   Patricia Minnegerode = Arthur = Madeleine Grand
10th Earl   d. 1926   d. 1951   d. 1952

Charlotte = Yanni Petsopoulos   Desmond = Jennifer   Rosemary = The Count Lanza   Myles = Alison Sarah   Matthew Charles

Alexis   Natasha Harriet   Ricardo Aleramo   Frederick Chloe Harry

Appendix II

January 1927
SHE STOOPS TO CONQUER
by OLIVER GOLDSMITH
Produced by Miss Marjorie
Clarke-Jervoise
(*Given in the Corn Exchange Theatre,*
Chichester)

September 1927
A MIDSUMMER NIGHT'S DREAM
by WILLIAM SHAKESPEARE
Produced by Mr J. Brandon Thomas

December 1927
ALADDIN
Written and produced by
LORD BESSBOROUGH

January 1928
TRILBY
by GEORGE DU MAURIER
Produced by Mr Leonard Graves

September 1928
THE MERCHANT OF VENICE
by WILLIAM SHAKESPEARE
Produced by Mr Rupert Harvey

December 1928
BOX AND COX
ST GEORGE AND THE DRAGON
Produced by Mr Rupert Harvey

January 1929
THE CAT AND THE CHERUB
by C. B. FERNALD
Produced by Mr Rupert Harvey
and A PANTOMINE REHEARSAL
by CECIL CLAY
Produced by Mr Ralph Alderson

August 1929
KING HENRY IV (Part I)
by WILLIAM SHAKESPEARE
Produced by Mr Rupert Harvey

December 1929
A CHILDREN'S CABARET
THE BRASS DOOR KNOB
CRAZED
Produced by Lord Bessborough

January 1930
OUTWARD BOUND
by SUTTON VANE
Produced by Mr Rupert Harvey

September 1930
THE TAMING OF THE SHREW
by WILLIAM SHAKESPEARE
Produced by Miss Marjorie
Clarke-Jervoise

January 1931
HOW HE LIED TO HER HUSBAND
by GEORGE BERNARD SHAW
and THE YOUNGER GENERATION
by STANLEY HOUGHTON
Produced by Mr Rupert Harvey

March 1932
TWELFTH NIGHT
by WILLIAM SHAKESPEARE
Produced by Mr Rupert Harvey

January 1936
TOBIAS AND THE ANGEL
by JAMES BRIDIE
Produced by Mr E. Martin Browne

September 1936
THE WINTER'S TALE
by WILLIAM SHAKESPEARE
Produced by Mr E. Martin Browne

January 1937
LABURNUM GROVE
by J. B. PRIESTLEY
Produced by Ralph Alderson

September 1937
LOVE'S LABOUR'S LOST
by WILLIAM SHAKESPEARE
Produced by Mr Rupert Harvey

September 1938
SCHOOL FOR SCANDAL
by R. B. SHERIDAN
Produced by Mr Robert Speaight

The following took part in the plays:
Mr Ralph Alderson
Miss Beryl Allen
Mr Guy Allen
Miss Gwendolen Armstrong-Jones
Miss Dulcie Bailey
Mr P. Baker
Mr Mark Baring
Mr Patrick Baring
Mr R. A. Barnes-Gorell
Sir Basil Bartlett
Mrs M. J. Bartlett
Mr K. S. Leith Bell
The Earl of Bessborough
Mr H. Bignold
Mr Simon Birch
Lady Susan Birch
Mr Wyndham Birch
Mr Maurice Blaze
Mrs Bollam
Mr John Booth
Miss Polly Booth
Mr Richard Border
Mr Guy Branch
Mr Michael Branch
Mr E. Brickhurst
The Hon. Geoffrey Browne
Mr E. Martin Browne
Mr H. Browning
Mr W. C. Browning
The Hon. Denys Buckley
The Hon. Mrs Buckmaster
Viscountess Buckmaster
Miss Cynthia Cadogan
Miss Patricia Cadogan
Mr John Cavanagh
Mr T. Chignell
Lady George Cholmondeley

Maj. A. F. Clarke-Jervoise
Miss Kathleen Cole
Mr W. T. Cole
The Lady Irene Congreve
Miss Deirdre Crauford
Mr J. R. Crichton
Mr Arthur Darley
Maj. T. W. G. Davis
Mr Andrew Duncan-Jones
Mr David Duncan-Jones
Mr Eady
Mr H. Farlow
Mr H. Ferrand
Miss Anne Flower
Mrs Neville Flower
Miss Dorothy Freshwater
The Hon. Mrs Gordon-Ives
Mr Victor Gordon-Ives
Mr Leonard Graves
Mr Ashworth Hall
Mr Rupert Harvey
Mr William Hickling
Mr Frank Holliman
Mr A. C. Hordern
Mr P. Hordern
Miss Ruth Hordern
Mrs Henry Howard
Miss Catherine Hunt
Miss Ruth Hunt
Cdr. J. F. Hutchings
Mrs Arthur James
The Rev. E. G. Langdale
Mr Hubert Langley
Mr Rupert Langley
Mr Percy Lee
Mr Bernard Lewis
Mr G. Lockhart
Capt. H. W. Luttman-Johnson

Miss Helen Mackay
Miss Jean Meade
Mr Nicholas Meredith
Mr Jean Louis de Neuflize
Mr Hardwick Nichols
Mr W. R. Nichols
Lady Caroline Paget
Miss Penelope Pike
Mr David Pike
Mr Arthur Ponsonby
The Lady Moyra Ponsonby
Mr C. Purver
Miss Allison Purves
Miss Henzie Raeburn
Mr Hilary Saunders
Miss Margaretta Scott
Mr Edward Selwyn
Miss Lucy Selwyn
Mr Arthur Slater
Miss Bridget Smiley
Miss Juliana Snell
Miss Anne Somerset
Mr Oliver Stedall
Mr Andrew Stephenson
Mr Wilfrid Stephenson
Mr A. L. Crampton Stewart
The Hon. Mrs Sturdy
Mr Eric Sutton
Mr F. Sweetman
Mr Humphrey Tilling
Mr Gerald Tomalin
Mr Tony Tomalin
Miss Margaret Vesey
Mrs E. H. Weller-Poley
Mr John Weller-Poley
Miss Sheila Weller-Poley

Mr Humphrey Whitbread
Miss Peggie White
Mr H. Wilson Wiley
Mr Arthur Willey
Mr John Woolfries
Miss Lilian Woolfries
Miss Winnie Woolfries
Miss Katherine Wyld
Mr Mansell Young

Members of the orchestra included:
Mr R. G. Border
Mr W. P. Breach
Miss D. Buckle
Mr T. Clarke
Mr G. Cole
Mrs D. Cox
Mrs N. H. Cox
Mrs E. V. Dawe
Miss F. Dawe
Mr G. Diggens
Mr F. J. Elderton
Miss A. Farne
Mr R. Floyd
Mrs A. Goodger
Mrs Harvey Grace
Mr D. Graves
Mr J. W. Hopkins
Mr J. Horton
Miss G. B. Keller
Mr L. Lewis
Mrs O. W. Lewis
Mr Percy Lewis
Mrs Percy Lewis
Mr Denis Mulgan
Miss L. O. Munro
Miss Margaret Pink
Mr G. Pyman
Mrs J. A. Richards
Mr E. Shepherd
Mr H. Sherwood
Mrs H. Sherwood
Mrs M. G. Steward
Miss M. Steward
The Rev. G. Street

Appendix III THE PRINCIPAL PICTURES

BARNEY, Joseph: The Show Man, 29 × 24 in.
Exhibited: Royal Academy, 1798, no. 457
Engraved: pub. by J. Young, 15 June 1797, with dedication to Lady Duncannon
The Young Pedlar, signed and dated 1798, 29 × 24 in.
Exhibited: Royal Academy, 1798, no. 138

BIRLEY, Sir Oswald: Roberte, Countess of Bessborough and her three children, the Viscount Duncannon, the Hon. Desmond Ponsonby and Lady Moyra Ponsonby, signed and dated 1922, 66 × 55 in.

BOGDANI, Jakob and Workshop: Partridge and other Birds, 39 × 48 in. A variant of a picture in the Royal Collection

BOURGEOIS, Sir Peter Francis: William, 2nd Earl of Bessborough distributing alms, 47 × 64 in.
Exhibited: Royal Academy, 1798, no. 4 'A nobleman relieving the poor with a view of Portland-road turnpike'

CAMPIDOGLIO, attributed to Michelangelo di: A Cockatoo and a Monkey with other birds, 38 × 46 in.

CASTEELS, Pieter: The Vain Jackdaw, signed and dated 1728, 49 × 40 in.
Fowls in Parks, one signed and dated 1730, a pair, 17 × 26 in.
A Peacock and Poultry in a Farmyard, 18 × 23½ in.

CATTERSON SMITH, Stephen, Snr: John William, 4th Earl of Bessborough, in the robes of the Order of Saint Patrick, 49 × 39½ in. A replica is in Dublin Castle.

COPLEY, John Singleton: William, 2nd Earl of Bessborough, 38 × 31 in. Another version of this portrait, signed

and dated 1790 and measuring 23 × 18¾ in., is in the Fogg Art Museum. An autograph replica was engraved in 1794 when in the possession of the sitter's friend, the 4th Earl of Clanbrassil, and is now at Milton. The portrait is based on that of Bessborough on the extreme right of the *Death of Lord Chatham* of 1779–81 in the Tate Gallery. Bessborough's is one of the likenesses classified as 'good' in an article in *The Gazeteer*, 5 May 1781

COTES, Francis: Lady Catherine Beauclerk, *née* Ponsonby, later Duchess of St Albans, signed and dated 1764, pastel, 23½ × 17¼ in.
Lady Charlotte Ponsonby, later Countess Fitzwilliam, signed and dated 1764, pastel, 23 × 17½ in.
Literature: E. M. Johnson, *Francis Cotes*, no. 138

CRADOCK, Marmaduke: A Peacock and Fowl in a Landscape, 39 × 49 in.

DALENS, Dirk: Arcadian Landscapes, one signed (4)

DANCE, attributed to Sir Nathaniel: Country House in a Park

EDWARDS, John: 10th Earl and Countess of Bessborough, with a Parrot, signed, 86 × 46 in.

ENGLISH SCHOOL, *circa* 1620: Henry Ponsonby of Hale, on panel, 14¾ × 11¾ in. Father of the following

FLEMISH SCHOOL, *circa* 1630: Sir John Ponsonby of Hale and Bessborough, on panel, 28½ × 21 in.

FUCHS, Emil: Blanche, Countess of Bessborough, crayon, 39 × 26 in.
Edward, 8th Earl of Bessborough, signed and dated 1907, crayon, 39 × 26 in.

GANDY, John: Portrait of an Officer, called John, Duke of Marlborough, 50 × 37¾ in.

GERMAN SCHOOL, 18th century: Hunting Party, on copper, 17 × 27 in.

GILBERT: Roberte, Countess of Bessborough, pastel

HOLBEIN, follower of Hans: Portrait of a man, called Thomas Cromwell, panel, 18 × 15 in.

HOPPNER, John: Henrietta Frances, Viscountess of Duncannon, later Countess of Bessborough, and her sons, John William, later 4th Earl of Bessborough and the Hon. Frederick Cavendish Ponsonby, 56 × 44 in.
Exhibited: Royal Academy, British Portraits, 1956, no. 359
Literature: W. Mackay & W. Roberts, *John Hoppner, R.A.*, 1914, p. 70
Finished before 1 June 1787 when the mezzotint by J. Young was published with a dedication to Lady Duncannon: a sketch or replica was in the artist's sale, Christie's, 31 May 1823, part of lot 26. The children were born respectively in 1781 and 1783

HUDSON, Thomas: The Rt Hon. John Ponsonby, Speaker of the Irish House of Commons, 1756, 50 × 40 in.
Younger son of the 1st Earl of Bessborough

HUET, Jean Baptiste: A Mallard and a Muscovy Duck among Flowers, signed and dated 1790, 21 × 53 in.

JACK, Richard: The Opening of Parliament, February 1932, signed and dated 1932, 49½ × 43 in.

JONGHERS, Alphonse: Vere, 9th Earl of Bessborough, in Garter robes, signed and dated 1935, 46 × 35 in.
Frederick, Viscount Duncannon

KAUFFMANN, Angelica: Georgiana, Duchess of Devonshire, 28 × 23½ in.
Provenance By descent to Claude A. C. Ponsonby, Christie's, 28 March 1908, lot 19 (70 gns, to Nosi)
The view of Tivoli established that this picture, and presumably the pendant, was painted during the

Duchess' visit to Italy

Henrietta Frances, Countess of Bessborough, 28 × 23½ in.
Provenance By descent to Claude A. C. Ponsonby, Christie's, 20 March 1908, lot 18 (100 gns. to Lord Bessborough)
Literature: Lady Victoria Manners & G. C. Williams, *Angelica Kauffmann*, 1924, p. 181
The two Spencer sisters were first painted with their brother by Angelica in the late 1760s: the picture is in a private collection. The full length portrait of the three at Althorp is of 1771

KICK, Cornelis: Tulips in a Vase, signed and dated 1670, 17 × 12 in.

LASZLO, Philip de: Vere, 9th Earl of Bessborough

LATILLA, Eugenio H.: The Hon. Frederick Ponsonby, later 6th Earl of Bessborough and the Hon. Augusta Ponsonby, later Countess of Kerry, 35¼ × 26¾ in.

LAWRENCE, Sir Thomas: Maria, Viscountess Duncannon, later Countess of Bessborough, 92 × 57 in.
Literature: K. Garlick, *A catalogue of the paintings, drawings and pastels of Sir Thomas Lawrence*, 1964, pp. 78–9, 270 and 293
Lady Maria Fane married Lord Duncannon in 1805 and the fact that she is referred to by her maiden name in the list of pictures prepared by Lawrence in February 1806, implies that the portrait was begun before her marriage: a first payment of £84 had been made. Lawrence's executors' list, no. 199, establishes that the picture was then abandoned: 'Head finished & figure partly sketched whole length'. The picture was reclaimed by Lord Duncannon, 12 July 1830 and finished by another hand

LELY, attributed to Sir Peter: Elizabeth, daughter of 1st Viscount Duncannon, wife of Stephen Moore and Thomas Newcomen, 50 × 40½ in.

LIOTARD, Jean Etienne: Hon. William Ponsonby, later 2nd Earl of Bessborough, in Turkish dress; and Lady Caroline Ponsonby, later Countess of Bessborough, in Venetian dress, a pair, 50 × 40 in.
Exhibited: Royal Academy, 1954, *European Masters of the 18th Century,* no. 407 and 405 *Literature:* R. Loche and M. Roethlisberger, *Liotard,* 1978, no. 48 and 49
Generally dated 1742–3, after the artist's return from the Levant, where he had been taken by the sitter in 1737

Frederick, Viscount Duncannon, later 3rd Earl of Bessborough, pastel, 24½ × 20 in.
Literature: Loche and Roethlisberger, 292
One of the series of portraits of the family executed in 1773–4 during Liotard's last visit to London, to which the two following pastels belong

William, Brabazon Ponsonby, later 1st Baron Ponsonby, signed and dated 1774, pastel, 24½ × 20 in.
Provenance: Vicomtess Vigier, Paris Galliera, 2 June 1970, where bought for Lord Bessborough
Literature: Loche and Roethlisberger, 306
The sitter was the 2nd Earl's nephew

George Ponsonby, later Lord Chancellor of Ireland, pastel, 24½ × 20 in.
Provenance: Claude Ponsonby, Christie's 28 March 1908, lot 8 (28 gns). to Lord Bessborough)
Literature: Loche and Roethlisberger, 309
The younger brother of the preceding

La Chocolatière *by Liotard.*

Princess Amelia, daughter of King George II, pastel, 24½ × 21 in.
Literature: Loche and Roethlisberger, 304

La Chocolatière: A Dutch Girl at Breakfast, 18¼ × 16¾ in.
Provenance: The artist's sale, Christie's 16 April 1774, lot 33
Exhibited: London, Royal Academy, *European Masters of the 18th Century,* 1954, no. 47
Literature: Loche and Roethlisberger, 57
Dated 1742–5 by Loche and Roethlisberger and to Liotard's first Dutch sojourn of 1755–6 by Staring: the picture on the wall is evidently by de Witte

LOCATELLI, Andrea: Italian Landscape, 38½ × 28½ in.

PHILIPS, attributed to Charles: Princess Amelia, daughter of King George II,

OPPOSITE *John William, 4th Earl of Bessborough, by Stephen Catterson-Smith, Jnr.*

92 × 57 in.
Probably based on a prototype by J. B.
van Loo

PHILLIPS, attributed to Thomas: John
William, 4th Earl of Bessborough,
29 × 24 in.

PHILPOT, Glyn W.: Loelia Ponsonby,
Duchess of Westminster, signed,
88 × 48 in.

PIPER, John: Chichester Cathedral,
watercolour and bodycolour,
26 × 30 in.

REYNOLDS, Sir Joshua: Henrietta Frances,
Viscountess Duncannon, later
Countess of Bessborough, 29 × 24 in.
The prototype of 1785 is at Althorp

ROBERTS, Ellis: Blanche, Countess of
Bessborough, 29 × 24 in.

ROMNEY, George: Charles, 3rd Duke of
Richmond, 29 × 24 in.
The prime version of this type is at
Goodwood: sittings are recorded in
1776 and 1777 and the pictures was
engraved by Watson in 1778. Copies
were painted for several of the Duke's
friends: five were paid for by the Duke
21 March 1777

RUBENS, follower of Sir Peter Paul: King
Solomon and the Queen of Sheba,
sketch, 19 × 24½ in.

RUSSELL, attributed to John: Frederick,
3rd Earl of Bessborough, pastel,
13¼ × 10¼ in.

SARGENT, John Singer: Vere, 9th Earl of
Bessborough; and Roberte, Countess
of Bessborough, both signed and dated
1913, crayon, 24 × 19 in.

SPENCER, Lavinia, Countess: Henrietta
Frances, Viscountess Duncannon,
later Countess of Bessborough, pen
and brown ink, grey wash,
12 × 18½ in.

STRANOVER, Tobias: Exotic Birds in a
Park, 62 × 54 mm.

STRANOVER, attributed to Tobias: A
Cockatoo and other Birds,
38½ × 33½ in.

THADDEUS, Henry Jones: Walter, 7th Earl
of Bessborough, signed, 49 × 39¼ in.

VAN DER GUCHT, Benjamin: Equestrian
Portrait of Frederick 3rd Earl of
Bessborough, signed and dated 1776,
35 × 29 in.
Provenance: Claude Ponsonby,
Christie's 28 March 1908, lot 42 (65
gns. to Lord Bessborough)

VAN DYCK, circle of Sir Anthony: Lady
Jane Brabazon, with inscription and
date 1617, 57 × 37 in.
Presumably Jane Bingley, who
married William Brabazon, later 1st
Earl of Meath in 1607. Mary, 1st
Viscountess Duncannon, was their
great-grand-daughter

VAN KESSELL, Jan: The Singing Lesson:
An Assembly of Birds, on panel,
10 × 13¾ in.
An Assembly of Birds, on panel,
14½ × 25 in.

VAN LOO, circle of: Town: and Country,
a pair

VAN LOO, attributed to Louis Michel:
Marquis et Marquise de Brienne, a
pair

VERNET, Claude Joseph: Mediterranean
Coast Scene with Fishermen, signed
and dated 1770, 28 × 38 in.
Executed in Paris, where Vernet
settled in 1762

WEENIX, attributed to Jan: Birds in a
Park, 18½ × 24 in.

WYNTRACK, Dirk: Poultry in a Farmyard,
on panel, a pair, 12½ × 16½ in.

ZEZZOS, Alexandro: Blanche, Countess of
Bessborough

OPPOSITE *The foot of the Staircase showing some
of the bird pictures.*

Appendix IV TWO SERMONS PREACHED IN STANSTED CHAPEL

Address given by the Bishop of Chichester, the Right Reverend E. W. Kemp, DD, at the dedication of the Banner of the European Parliament in Stansted Chapel, Sussex, 27 April 1975

'And the whole earth was of one language and of one speech'
Genesis XI. 1.

THESE WORDS INTRODUCE the story of the Tower of Babel which is one of that group of myths and folk-tales which make up the earlier chapters of the Book of Genesis. Like the others it raises a number of historical difficulties and contains very rudimentary and child-like conceptions of the deity, but also, like the other early narratives it conveys certain spiritual lessons which can be related to what is found in other parts of the Bible. The story emphasises the supremacy of God over the whole world, it teaches that mankind is in the divine creation essentially one, and that the divisions and hostilities and among men arise from their overweening ambition and pride, from trying to put themselves in the place of God.

This emphasis on the essential unity of mankind might seem at first sight inconsistent with the prominence and special relationship to God assigned to the Hebrew people in the rest of the Old Testament, but properly understood this is not so. The choice and calling of the Hebrews, it is emphasized, was not through any merit of their own, nor was it to make them superior to other people, but in order that they might be an instrument through which the knowledge of God should be spread throughout the world and all mankind come to worship and serve him. The culmination of this in the coming of Christ to begin a new creation in which, as St Paul writes to the Galatians, there is no such thing as Jew and Greek 'for you are all one person in Christ Jesus'.

The unity of mankind is based upon the fact of our creation by the one God and it will only be perfectly realised when all men truly accept the reign of Christ and are changed into his likeness. So much is essential to Christian belief, but it does not follow that all we have to do is to preach the Gospel and then international peace and order will follow. That is in principle the same mistake as has been made at times by some Christian movements whose leaders have seemed to suggest that social and industrial conflict could be settled by the conversion of individuals. This is to ignore the fact that charity is built upon justice. In traditional Christian moral teaching there are seven virtues. Four of them, the so called cardinal virtues of prudence, temperance, fortitude and justice are shared by Christianity with many other ethical systems. The other three, the theological virtues of faith, hope and love, are more specially the contribution of Christianity. They transform and perfect the cardinal virtues, but they do not supersede them. So it is a part of our duty in thinking about the unity of mankind to study the application of the cardinal virtues and other such principles to the problem of human divisions and to bring to bear whatever can be learned from social psychology, economics and other techniques. Christians should be aware of high sounding language which is not based upon knowledge.

Interior of the Chapel.

It is, for example, futile to talk of the unity of mankind or of world citizenship and at the same time to ignore or depreciate the importance of associations such as the nation or the state in the lives of human beings. We need, perhaps, to be reminded that nation and state are not the same thing. The state is an association of persons viewed from the standpoint of public order. It exists to provide that degree of security without which the continuance of human life and society are impossible. The nation is related rather to race and culture. It furnishes a man with an environment which, as it has been said, keeps him from becoming a physical and moral nomad. It gives him a milieu to provide the physical, moral and intellectual nourishment necessary for his life. It is one of the factors which minister to the formation of human character, one very important factor, just as the family on a smaller scale is another. In our thinking about international order we must recognize this importance of nationality in relation to human character. Men need these smaller associations in the development of their personality, and it is wrong that they should be ignored or suppressed.

Christian moral teaching has recognized the value of both state and nation, and the place that they have in the divine ordering of the world, but it has also insisted that both are subordinate to international order. It is remarkable that in a period when the Church itself was breaking up, in the sixteenth and seventeenth centuries, there should have come from the separated parts of it a striking unanimity of testimony to the Christian and moral bases of international order and unity. The Dominican theologian, Francis de Vitoria, the Spanish Jesuit Suarez and the Dutch Calvinist Grotius are principal figures among those who, in the sixteenth and seventeenth centuries, developed ideas of Roman lawyers and Christian Fathers into the foundations of modern international law. Vitoria, for example, in language which is at times surprisingly modern, argued for the freedom of the sea and freedom of trade as natural rights, and condemned the Spanish Conquest of Mexico as a violation of the rights of the Mexicans to govern themselves in their own way. He also condemned the forcible conversion of the Mexicans and their baptism by the Spanish Jesuits. Grotius, a lawyer as well as a theologian, and indeed better as a lawyer than a theologian, is the acknowledged father of international law, but this eminence should not be allowed to obscure the fact that he is one among other figures in a broad Christian tradition.

That tradition asserts that there are principles of order in creation – what is sometimes called natural law – whose recognition by men and states is necessary for the survival of the human race in anything that could be called a civilized condition. It is a matter for interest and thankfulness that whereas twenty-five years ago or less any mention of natural law would have been greeted with sceptical smiles by most of our university philosophers, there has in this last quarter of a century been a great revival of concern for the subject and a realization that it may be of fundamental importance for us.

In England this revival is in part due to the writings of Professor Herbert Hart whose book *The Concept of Law* published in 1961 has been of very great influence in the schools of law and philosophy. Professor Hart is Jewish in origin, and, I believe, an agnostic, and that in itself stresses the importance of natural law as a uniting factor among people of differing outlooks – something relevant to the fact that the newer states of Africa and Asia and the Communist states are understandably suspicious of an international law whose principles have been so demonstrably formulated by the Christian countries of Europe. We must therefore be careful to insist that these principles, though illuminated by the Christian revelation, rest upon something antecedent to it – upon what Christians might call the doctrine of creation and others rational reflection on the nature of man. We must show that there is a common ground, a meeting place.

European unity ought to be seen in this broad setting. It would be regrettable if the present economic crisis caused the debate about the EEC to be dominated by economic arguments. In one sense we are all Marxists nowadays – we all acknowledge the powerful influence of economic factors in human history. But economics is not an exact science. I remember some years ago hearing from one of my colleagues who was in the Faculty of PPE that there had had, through illness, to be a change of examiner in the economics section of the Final Honour School, after the papers had been set, and one of the economics papers had to be re-set because the new examiner could not understand his predecessor's questions. We must look at the European question in larger perspective than that of economics, and see European unity, even within the limited area of the EEC, as helping towards the greater unity of mankind and the establishment of that rule of law and that order among states which will enable men best to grow and to live their lives as God means them to do. The recent Lomé agreement between the EEC and so many states of the 'Third World' is real evidence of the desire of the members of the Community to look outwards and to make the Community serve all men. The very fact of the binding together in one community of states which have behind them centuries of armed conflict culminating in the two World Wars is another evidence of the contribution of the EEC to world order and peace.

But it is permissible and right that we should look at European unity also from another point of view – and in relation to what I said earlier about nations as providing men with an environment which keeps them from being physical and moral nomads. Europe provides the main part of our cultural environment. The ease and speed of modern communications can convey in more tangible form to this generation that sense of belonging to Europe which the knowledge of our history has always given. At the end of his great book on *The Making of Europe* (1935) Christopher Dawson writes:

> It is well to remember that the unity of our civilisation does not rest entirely on the secular culture and the material progress of the last four centuries. There are deeper traditions in Europe than these, and we must go back behind Humanism and behind the superficial triumphs of modern civilisation if we wish to discover the fundamental social and spiritual forces that have gone to the making of Europe.

Among these forces due place must be given to that tradition of prayer, manual work, study and ordered life in community which has existed from the time of St Benedict in the sixth century and which through the Dark Ages also preserved for us the basic elements of classical culture, ensuring that our roots go back beyond the Middle Ages into Greece and Rome. It was a right instinct which led the present Pope to proclaim St Benedict the patron saint of Europe.

But there are other expressions of these 'fundamental social and spiritual forces'. Sir Richard Southern writing (in *The Making of the Middle Ages*, 1953) of the battle of Roncevaux in 778 and its place in the popular memory enshrined in one of the great medieval epics *The Song of Roland*, says that it was a defeat with no military significance, but it appealed to those qualities which held men together throughout Europe: 'personal valour, faithfulness to lord and companions, and confidence in the Christian religion and in the aid of the saints. Other loyalties were to be added in due course, but these were the basis of all else'. 'Personal valour, faithfulness to lord and companions, and confidence in the Christian religion and in the aid of the saints': that is, we might say, courage in the face of difficulty, adversity and danger; trustworthiness involving integrity and reliability towards those with whom we live and work and care for them; sure faith in Christ with a confidence in his victory over evil and the certainty of the ultimate triumph of good; the sense of belonging to a great community of faithful men and women extending through the ages and of receiving from them a heritage which they look to us to care and to pass on to our children. These are essentials of the European tradition, which we look for European unity to maintain and to contribute to that greater unity of the nations for which we pray.

Resumé of sermon preached by the Reverend Canon R. T. Greenacre, Chancellor of Chichester Cathedral, at St Paul's Chapel, Stansted Park, on 25 January (The Conversion of St Paul), 1981

1. My happiness at being with you on this occasion of double celebration – both your Feast of Title (St Paul) and your Feast of Dedication (anniversary of consecration of 25 January 1819).

2. So first of all today we must take a look at the personality of St Paul.

(a) Not at first sight a popular of lovable figure: querulous, over-sensitive, apparently something of a misogynist. To many, the man who complicated the 'simple Gospel' of Jesus with subtle theologizing – but this view will not survive serious examination.

(b) The Conversion of St Paul was in fact a crucial turning point in the history of the Church; it turned the Church from a minority sect within Judaism into – potentially at least – the Catholic (i.e. universal) Church.

(c) Paul was a man whose intellect was passionately on fire for Christ. Many people are passionate in their emotions; intellectual passion is rarer. That passion fires all his writings and gives his *Letters* their lasting value.

(d) *The Division of the Apostolate*: Peter 'Apostle to the Circumcision', Paul, 'Apostle of the Gentiles'. Paul was the first to see with total clarity the implications of the Gospel claim that Jesus is Lord and to spell them out.

(e) The paradox of Paul's own 'Jewishness'. He took the lead in welcoming Gentiles as equal partners into the Church and vigorously and he sharply opposed the 'judaizing' party in the Church, yet he himself was unashamedly proud of his own background and pedigree and held up for his readers a vision of the permanent and abiding vision of Israel. In chapters 9–11 of the *Letter to the Romans* he agonizes over the mystery of Israel. Read *Romans* chapter 11, verses 25–33:

> Lest you be wise in your own conceits, I want you to understand this mystery, brethren: a hardening has come upon part of Israel, until the full number of the Gentiles come in, and so all Israel will be saved; as it is written,
> 'The Deliverer will come from Zion, he will banish ungodliness from Jacob';
> 'and this will be my covenant with them when I take away their sins.'
> As regards the gospel they are enemies of God, for your sake; but as regards election they are beloved for the sake of their forefathers. For the gifts and the call of god are irrevocable. Just as you were once disobedient to God but now have received mercy because of their disobedience, so they have now been disobedient in order that by the mercy shown to you they also may receive mercy. For God has consigned all men to disobedience, that he may have mercy upon all.
> O the depth of the riches and wisdom and knowledge of God! How unsearchable are his judgements and how inscrutable his ways!

3. I turn now from St Paul, the man whose letters form so crucial a part of the New Testament and who is honoured and celebrated in *all* the Churches, to a comparatively obscure English clergyman. To quote the Consecration Service of this Chapel in 1819 it 'pleased (God) to put it into the heart of his servant, the Reverend Lewis Way, MA, to erect this House to his honour and glory.' I have a feeling that it is because of Lewis Way that I am here today, for in different ways Lord Bessborough and I are both his successors – Lord Bessborough as the owner of Stansted Park and myself as former chaplain of the church he founded in Paris in 1824.

Until a week ago I had not taken Lewis Way too seriously. I thought of him as an amiable eccentric of great wealth, with that not uncommon combination (even today) of piety and dottiness; the man who built this Chapel, founded the English Church (and built the Boulevard des Anglais) in Nice, and then founded the Marbœuf Chapel, now St George's Church, in Paris; a man who had a bee in his bonnet about the conversion of the Jews (hence the extraordinary east window in this Chapel) and their return to Palestine. But last week I was lent a quite fascinating document, *Mémoires sur l'Etat des Israélites*, a dossier he presented to the Tsar of All the Russias in 1818 and then in the following year to the Foreign Ministers of Russia, Austria, Prussia and England at the Congress of Aix-le-Chapelle. In it is to be found –

(i) An apocalyptic and fundamentalist element that is quite foreign to us today and could make us dismiss the whole case as fantastic nonsense; a detailed interpretation of Old Testament prophecies and of the Revelation to John in the light of the cataclysmic events of the French Revolution.

(ii) But also an extraordinary positive grasp of several points of fundamental importance for Christian-Jewish relations:

(a) The sinfulness of Christian persecution of the Jews. 'If in a former epoch', he writes, 'they (the Jews) had felt moved by the desire to have a closer look at the claim of Jesus to be their Messiah, would they have been able to recognize the imprint of his character in the conduct of his avowed disciples? . . . could they have found it in the jails of the Inquisition or in the camps of a Crusade? Could they have hoped for deliverance from these Pharaohs of modern Egypt. these Sennacheribs of a mystical Babylon.'

This was a message that should have been heeded, but a continuing Christian anti-semitism helped to make Hitler's genocide possible. We need in this context to remember the protest of Léon Bloy against Christian involvement in the Dreyfus affair. 'Antisemi-tism . . . is the most horrible blow which Our Lord has received in his passion that con-tinues for ever: it is the most bloody and unpardonable because he receives it on the face of his Mother and from the hands of Christians.'

(b) The need to accord Jews full and equal rights as citizens in the countries of Europe and at the same time to recognize their own national identity.

(c) For Christians the Jews have not ceased to be God's people. For a while they are estranged from us but their destiny is still bound up with ours and there is a long term hope of their final reconciliation. To Lewis Way this hope was conditional upon the return of the Jews to Palestine.

4. To conclude, is there anything we can deduce from the very different vocations of Paul, the Jewish Apostle to the Gentiles, and Lewis Way, a Gentile Apostle to the Jews? Surely at least one thing: that the unity of the Christian Church is not an end in itself, but only a means to, a sign of, the unity of all mankind in Christ.

Appendix V STANSTED: SALIENT DATES

The nearest known Roman remains in Watergate Hanger are no longer visible. In late Saxon times 'Stanestede', in the Forest of Bere, represented the whole or part of 16 hides of Stoughton held by Earl Godwin of King Edward the Confessor.

1052   **Godwin** is thought to have made Stansted his base from which he made descents on the Isle of Wight.

1066   After the Norman Conquest, the same hides were temporarily attached to Westbourne.

1086   In Domesday Book they were included in the Hundred of Bourne. During the 11th century a hunting lodge was probably built for **Roger de Montgomery**, 1st Earl of Arundel.

1094   **Roger de Montgomery** dies.

1102   His successor, **Robert de Bellême**, is attainted and forfeits his estates.

1138   **William d'Aubigny** becomes Earl of Arundel.

1176   **William d'Aubigny** dies.

1177   **Henry II**, intending to sail for Normandy but finding winds unfavourable, comes to Stansted where he hears that the Papal Legate threatens to place the kingdom under interdict unless he permits consummation of the marriage of his son, **Richard the Lionheart**, with **Alice**, daughter of the **King of France**.

1179   **Richard** and **Ralph**, the King's falconers, are at Stansted.

1181   **Silvester** and his comrades look after the King's birds.

1181–84   The first recorded dwellings on the site of the present chapel are built for **Henry II**, who stays on various occasions while rebuilding the Roman fort at Portchester or waiting to sail for France. Stone of this date is said to exist in a buttress at the north-east end of the Chapel.

1194   **Richard the Lionheart** hunts deer and wild boar at Stansted.

1214   **King John** is at Stansted before setting out to invade Poitou.

1215   **King John** again at Stansted some six months before he signed Magna Carta at Runnymede, orders a cask of wine at Aldingbourne.

1244   Stansted, becoming part of the dower granted by **Hugh**, last d'Aubigny Earl, to his sister and co-heir, **Isabel**, Countess of Arundel, passes to her son, **John Fitzalan**, Earl of Arundel and Chief Butler to the King.

1283   During the minority of **Richard**, 3rd Fitzalan Earl, the Manor is granted with Westbourne to the Abbey of Vale Royal.

1297   **Edward I** passes through Stansted on his way from Bedhampton to Arundel.

1302–30   Stansted forms part of the Manor of Westbourne.

1306   **William de Whiteway** trespasses in the park, is convicted before the Treasurer and Barons of the Exchequer and committed to the Tower of London.

1327   A Survey describes Stansted as

comprising 'a hall, two chambers with a Chapel, a kitchen and a chamber over the gate, a stable and a cowshed beyond reprises'.

1335 **Richard**, 5th Fitzalan Earl, complains that 'divers persons broke into his parks ... and carried away deer' and 'that the **Dean of Chichester** ... cut down his trees and carried them away'

1411–12 According to a subsidy levied in these years: '**Thomas**, Earl of Arundel and Surrey has Arundel Castle, and has manors, lands, etc., viz., the Manor of Bourne with Stanstede, Walderton and the hundred, members of that manor: £53'.

1415 Probable military activity in preparation for the embarkation from Portchester of **Henry V's** army for Agincourt.

1422–55 Stansted is held in dower by **Eleanor**, widow of **John**, 8th Fitzalan Earl.

1480 The buildings restored for **Thomas**, Lord Maltravers, later 12th Earl of Arundel. The south porch and west door of the present Chapel are of this date.

1552 **Edward VI**, aged 15, visits Stansted.

1579 On the death of **Henry**, the last Fitzalan Earl, Stansted descends with Westbourne to his son-in-law, **John**, Lord Lumley, in right of his wife, **Jane**, **Henry's** daughter who died in 1576.

1581 'Wild beastes' are transferred from Goodwood and East Dean to Stansted.

1591 **Queen Elizabeth**, arriving at Stansted on her way to Portsmouth, said to have cried, 'Stand steed'.

1609 **John Lumley** is succeeded by his cousin, **Sir Richard Lumley**.

1617 His second wife, **Elizabeth**, daughter of **Baron d'Arcy**, dies, stating in her will: 'that Matthewes and his sonne have the same charge ... of these lands and libertyes and woods ... which heretofore and now presently they have, carrying themselves as they ought to doe'.

1626 **Sir Richard Lumley's** first wife, **Frances**, widow of **William Holland** of Chichester, is buried at Westbourne.

1628 **Richard Lumley** is created Viscount.

1643 Royalist commander, **Lord Hopton**, sends cavalry to attack Stansted in December.

1644 Parliamentary General, **Sir William Waller**, takes the place with '2000 horse and foot with two drakes' (a kind of small cannon) and largely destroys the castellated buildings of which the only remains are the south and west part of the Chapel.

1651 **Charles II**, passing through Stansted in October before escaping to France, meets **Colonel Gunter**, according to legend, in 'the central avenue of Stansted Forest'.

1661 **Lord Lumley** is succeeded by his grandson, another **Richard**.

1685 His troop of Sussex militia and Hampshire horse captures **Lord Grey** and the **Duke of Monmouth** in the New Forest a few days after the Battle of Sedgemoor.

1686 **Richard Lumley**, builds the first house on the present site.

1690 **Richard Lumley**, now Earl of Scarbrough, fights in the Battle of the Boyne, contributing to final Jacobite defeat.

1692 **William III** visits Stansted and

Lord Scarbrough is promoted Major-General.

1716   **The Prince of Wales**, later **George II**, stays on his way to Portsmouth to view fortifications and review regiments.

1722   **The Prince of Wales'** father, **George I**, visits Stansted and receives an address from the Corporation of Chichester.

1724   **Daniel Defoe** describes Stansted as 'a house seeming to be a retreat . . . surrounded with thick woods, through which . . . are the most . . . agreeable Vistos . . . anywhere in England.'

1739   **Richard**, 2nd Earl of Scarbrough, is succeeded by his brother **Thomas**, 3rd Earl, who, on the death of his cousin, **Thomas Saunderson**, assumes that name and inherits estates in Yorkshire, including Sandbeck.

1766   Stansted passes by will to **George Montague-Dunk**, 2nd Earl of Halifax, whose mother was **Mary Lumley**, eldest daughter of **Richard**, 1st Earl of Scarbrough. During his time Lumley Seat and Racton Tower were built.

1771   **Lord Halifax** dies leaving Stansted to his natural daughter **Anna Donaldson**, wife of **Richard Archdall**.

1778   After a visit by **George III** and **Queen Charlotte**, trustees put the Estate on the market.

1781   The Estate is sold to Indian Nabob, **Richard Barwell**, who summons **Capability Brown** to redesign the park and gardens.

1782   After **Brown's** death **Barwell** calls in **James Wyatt** and **Joseph Bonomi**. The old wings are removed and the house encased in white plaster. Two porticos and double Doric colon-

nades are added. **Grimm's** drawings of Stansted, Lordington and Racton Tower were done in this year before restoration of the main house.

1804   **Richard Barwell** dies. A monument by **Nollekens** is erected in Westbourne Church. The Estate is sold to **Lewis Way**.

1819   The Chapel, restored probably by **Thomas Hopper** who may also have designed the present stable block, is reconsecrated at a Service attended by **John Keats**.

1822   **Lewis Way**, failing in his scheme to transform Stansted into a college for the conversion of the Jews, winters abroad.

1826   **Lewis Way**, failing again to obtain a charter to turn Stansted into a college, sells the property to **Charles Dixon**, a London wine merchant and philanthropist.

1885   **Charles Dixon** dies, aged 84, and is buried in the Chapel.

1856   **Dixon's** stepson, **George Wilder**, dies at the age of 36 and is also buried in the Chapel.

1871   **Mrs Dixon** dies having devised the Estate in trust for her grandson, **George Wilder**, then only nine years old.

1887–9   The **Wilders** rent Stansted to **Admiral, the Earl Clanwilliam**, father of **Admiral Sir Herbert Meade-Fetherstonhaugh**, subsequent owner of Uppark.

1896   **George Wilder**, aged 46, dies of pneumonia on returning from yachting.

1900   The main block is destroyed by fire on the last day of Goodwood Races.

1903   The house is re-built by **Arthur Conran Blomfield**.

1912	**George Wilder** sells Stansted to **Major Cecil Whitaker**, who rents the house for a few years to **Captain Quintin Dick** and his widow who married **Lord Howe**.
1924	**Major Whitaker** sells Stansted to **Vere**, 9th Earl of Bessborough.
1926	The Chapel is restored by **H.S. Goodhart-Rendel**.
1927	The Stansted Theatre is built. During the following years **The Princess Royal** and the **Earl of Harewood** stay at Stansted for Goodwood Races.
1931–5	**Lord Bessborough** is Governor-General of Canada.
1939	**Queen Elizabeth**, wife of **George VI**, spends a night at Stansted and plants an oak tree.
1940	The Chapel is damaged by enemy action.
1942	The Stansted Theatre is burnt down.
1947	The Chapel is again restored by **H.S. Goodhart-Rendel**.
1948	**Lewis Way's** communion plate is returned to Stansted by St George's Church in Paris.
1956	**Vere**, 9th Earl of Bessborough, dies and is succeeded by **Frederick**, 10th and present Earl.
1957	The old stables are converted into a cricket pavilion.
1959	The old laundry and bakery become a bathing pavilion.
1962	**Princess Anne** comes over from Lordington to swim at Stansted.
1962–4	**Mr Peter Thorneycroft**, Minister of Defence, and **Mrs Thorneycroft** occupy the Clock Tower Flat, while **Lord Bessborough** is a Minister for Science.
1968	**Princess Alexandra** and the **Hon. Angus Ogilvy** visit Stansted for the Chichester Festival.
1970	**Lord Bessborough** is appointed Minister of State at the Ministry of Technology, and in
1973	Elected first British Vice-President of the European Parliament.
1981	**Prince and Princess Michael of Kent** visit Stansted for the Chichester Festival.
1983	The Stansted Park Foundation is formed.

Picture Credits

PICTURE SOURCES

Lord Bessborough: 1; 25; 32; 43; 48;
51 (both); 56; 59; 62; 63; 68; 85; 86;
87; 91; 93; 98 (both); 103; 105 (both);
107; 108; 109; 110; 111; 115 (both);
117 (both); 119 (both); 120 (left);
123; 125; 126; 132; 142.

The Marquess of Bath: 26.
British Library: 15; 19.
British Museum: 31; 65 (above); 74.
Chichester Cathedral: 21.
Chichester Festival Theatre: 129
(both).
Christie's: 67 (both); 106.
Fishbourne Roman Palace: 11.
National Buildings Record: 24.
National Motor Museum: 94; 95; 96.
National Portrait Gallery: 34; 45; 75.
Royal Institute of British Architects:
99.
The Earl of Scarbrough: 28; 29; 39.
Sotheby's: 17.

PHOTOGRAPHIC CREDITS

All colour plates were photographed
by Mark Fiennes unless otherwise
stated.

Bill Bates – Van Hallan: 120 (right)
Country Life: Jonathan M. Gibson: 33;
91; 105 (right).
Country Life: Alex Starkey: 18; 32; 41;
47; 49; 57; 62; 63; 65 (right); 77; 84;
101; 113; 147.
Mark Fiennes: 4–5; 35; 86; 87; 98
(right); 105 (left); 110; 111; 115
(both); 117 (both); 119 (both); 120
(left); 142.
A. F. Kersting: 2; 22; 79; 81; 98
(above); 135.
Angus McBean: 129 (left).
Eric S. Peacock: 9; 42; 133; 134.

Map, picture key and family trees on
pages 6–7, 124 and 136–37 by Heather
Sherratt.

Index

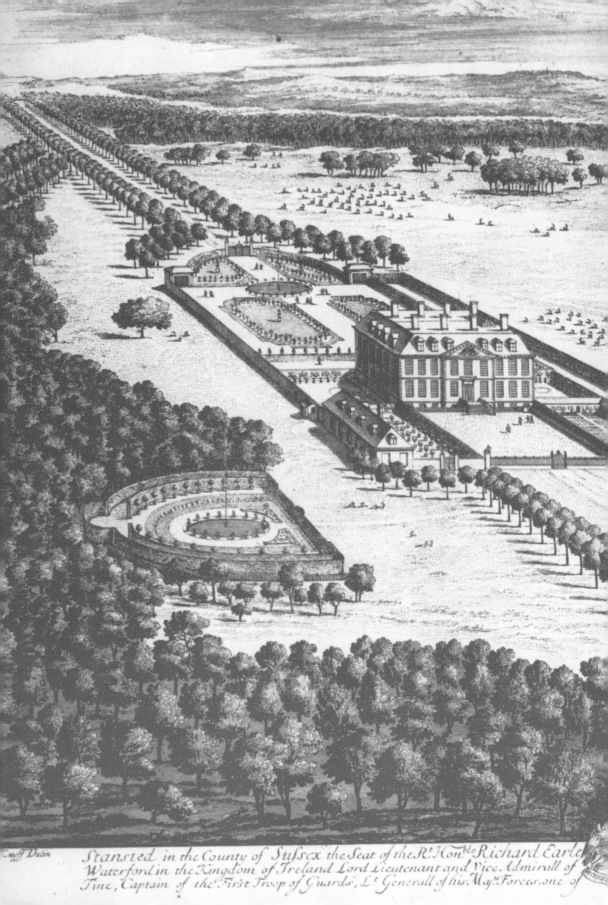

Stansted in the County of Sussex the Seat of the R.t Hon.ble Richard Earle
Waterford in the Kingdom of Ireland Lord Lieutenant and Vice Admirall of
Tine, Captain of the First Troop of Guards, L.t Generall of his May.ts Forces, one of